OXFORD THEOLOGICAL MONOGRAPHS

Oxford Theological Monographs

CANONS OF THE COUNCIL OF SARDICA

A.D. 343

A Landmark in the Early Development of Canon Law

By HAMILTON HESS. 1958

THE NEW TEMPLE

The Church in the New Testament

By R. J. MCKELVEY. 1968

NEW LITURGICAL FEASTS IN LATER MEDIEVAL ENGLAND

BY

R. W. PFAFF

OXFORD
AT THE CLARENDON PRESS
1970

Oxford University Press, Ely House, London W.1

GLASGOW NEW YORK TORONTO MELBOURNE WELLINGTON
CAPE TOWN SALISBURY IBADAN NAIROBI DAR ES SALAAM LUSAKA ADDIS ABABA
BOMBAY CALCUTTA MADRAS KARACHI LAHORE DACCA
KUALA LUMPUR SINGAPORE HONG KONG TOKYO

PRINTED IN GREAT BRITAIN

TO

MARGARET

PREFACE

THIS study deals with a number of new liturgical feasts which came to be accepted—or seem to have been in the process of being accepted—in England at the close of the middle ages. Of these the most important are the Transfiguration, the Visitation, and the Name of Jesus.[1] A chapter has been devoted to each, and another to four feasts only in the process of becoming established by the time of the Reformation changes: the Five Wounds, the Crown of Thorns, the Compassion of the Virgin, and her Presentation. The last chapter discusses in greater detail yet another 'incipient' feast, that of the 'Iconia Domini', about which very little has been known. Some general considerations are discussed in the introductory chapter, and in the conclusion an effort is made briefly to set the entire study in a wider context.

We are concerned here with the strictly liturgical: that is, feasts having a mass and/or office and finding, or being in the process of finding, a regular place in the sanctorale of the missal and breviary. We shall see that new feasts are of two classes: those which are 'liturgical' in origin—Transfiguration, Visitation, Presentation, Crown of Thorns, 'Iconia'—and those which seem to develop from devotions in private manuals or books of hours—Wounds, Compassion, and probably the Name of Jesus. Other devotions of this latter type, like the Joys of the Virgin or the Fifteen Oes, did not become liturgical (in England at any rate), and are not part of our concern. The area of private devotion, especially in so far as it takes poetic form, has been quite intensively studied, in contrast to the more liturgical aspects of late medieval spirituality. The emphasis here, then, is on specifically liturgical problems, particularly on the origin and spread of service forms, and on the pattern of acceptance which the new feasts found.

New feasts of saints have not been considered. Their spread, being often a matter of mere extension from local to provincial to national level or beyond is generally of less complexity, both

[1] These are sometimes referred to collectively as the principal 'nova festa'.

historically and theologically, than those of Christ and the Virgin; and their omission helps us to avoid the pitfalls of 'heortology', a fascinating but basically rather unreflective subject, usefully amassing pieces of evidence but too often without considering their setting and value.

An effort has been made to treat each chapter as more or less a self-contained unit. This involves some repetition in the descriptions of manuscripts and enumeration of early printed editions. But I have tried to keep such repetition to a minimum.

Since this work is intended primarily as a contribution to liturgical history rather than to paleography or the description of manuscripts, abbreviations and contractions have generally been expanded, though the original spelling and capitalization have on the whole been retained. I do not pretend to be skilled in the dating of scripts, and have had to rely in this matter on the consensus of scholars who are.

A study such as this must be based in the first instance on accepting as provisionally correct the descriptions of liturgical manuscripts contained in the principal relevant catalogues:[1] van Dijk (in typescript only) for the Bodleian, the various separate volumes for the British Museum, the six volumes (incomplete) of the Cambridge University Library manuscripts, the fine catalogues of M. R. James for the Cambridge colleges, and for the Oxford colleges the old work of Coxe (1852), supplemented by Frere's *Bibliotheca Musico-Liturgica* and, for the colleges which keep their manuscripts in the Bodleian, by van Dijk. (There are also separate modern catalogues for Balliol, Merton, and Christ Church.) Frere supplies some information about many of the Oxford and Cambridge manuscripts, as well as those of smaller collections throughout the British Isles, but his work omits the British Museum entirely. An intensely valuable conspectus is provided by the second edition (1964) of Ker's *Medieval Libraries of Great Britain*, which lists all manuscripts of which medieval ownership by some sort of institutional library can be traced. (Consequently, of course, some of the most valuable liturgical manuscripts are not included.) The capsulated descriptions in Ker are, for matters other than ownership, based partly on a new examination of the manu-

[1] Page numbers have generally not been given for these catalogues, because reference can quickly be found by use of the manuscript number.

scripts, partly on descriptions in the standard catalogues. Attributions for which Ker has not considered the evidence sufficiently strong he has sometimes queried, sometimes omitted, sometimes relegated to the category of 'rejected'.

Folio references to manuscripts cited have not been given when the reference is to a kalendar or martyrology, for any reader looking up a reference in them can quickly find the desired place on his own. It is hoped that the diminution of clutter in pages already crowded enough with necessary references will compensate for this inconsistency of citation. It should be remembered that, of the Oxford college manuscripts cited here, those of Brasenose, Corpus Christi, New, Trinity, and University Colleges are deposited in the Bodleian.

Help which I have received on specific points is acknowledged in the text. It is a pleasure to express my thanks for more general help to Dr. J. J. G. Alexander, the Revd. Dr. Henry Chadwick, Dr. R. W. Hunt, Dr. N. R. Ker, and Dr. A. C. de la Mare. The staff of Duke Humphrey's Library at the Bodleian have been especially patient and helpful. Finally I am much indebted to the erudition and interest of my mentor, the Revd. Dr. T. M. Parker.[1]

R. W. P.

Chapel Hill
December 1968

[1] Research grants from the University of North Carolina have materially aided in the preparation of this book.

CONTENTS

ABBREVIATIONS

AA. SS.	*Acta Sanctorum* (70 vols.; Antwerp, 1643–).
AHMA	*Analecta Hymnica Medii Aevi*, ed. G. M. Dreves and C. Blume (55 vols., Leipzig, 1886–1922).
Alc.	Alcuin Society Collections.
Backaert	Backaert, B. 'L'Évolution du Calendrier Cistercien', *Collectanea Ord. Cist. Ref.* xii (1950), 81–94, 302–16; xiii (1951), 107–27.
Bale, *Script.*	Bale, J., *Scriptorum Illustrium Maioris Brytanniae* (Basel, 1559).
Barking Ordinal	*Ordinale and customary of the Benedictine nuns of Barking abbey*, ed. J. B. L. Tolhurst (HBS lxv, 1927; lxvi, 1928).
Bäumer	Bäumer, S., *Histoire du bréviaire romain* (French tr., revised R. Biron, 2 vols., Paris, 1905).
Bonniwell	Bonniwell, W. R., *A History of the Dominican Liturgy* (New York, 1944).
Camd.	Camden Society, followed by series designation.
CE	*Catholic Encyclopedia* (15 vols., New York, 1907–14).
Ceremonies . . . of Salisbury	*Ceremonies and Processions of the Cathedral Church of Salisbury*, ed. C. Wordsworth (Cambridge, 1901).
Coll. Anglo-Prem.	*Collectanea Anglo-Premonstratensia*, ed. F. A. Gasquet (Camd. 3rd ser. vi, 1904; x, 1906; xii, 1906).
CPL	*Calendar of Papal Letters*, ed. W. H. Bliss and J. A. Twemlow (14 vols., London, 1904–61).
DACL	*Dictionnaire d'Archéologie Chrétienne et de Liturgie* (15 vols., Paris, 1907–53).
DHGE	*Dictionnaire d'Histoire et de Géographie Ecclésiastique* (Paris, 1912–).
DNB	*Dictionary of National Biography* (21 vols., London, 1908–9).
DTC	*Dictionnaire de Théologie Catholique* (15 vols., Paris, 1903–50).
van Dijk	Dijk, S. J. P. van, *Handlist of Latin Liturgical Manuscripts in the Bodleian Library* (7 vols., typed, 1953).

van Dijk and Walker	Dijk, S. J. P. van, and Walker, J. H., *Origins of the Modern Roman Liturgy* (London, 1960).
Dugdale	Dugdale, W., *Monasticon Anglicanum*, ed. J. Caley et al. (6 vols., London, 1813–30).
Ebner	Ebner, A., *Quellen und Forschungen . . . des Missale Romanum. Iter Italicum* (Freiburg, 1896).
EC	*Enciclopedia Cattolica* (12 vols., Rome, 1949–54).
EETS	Early English Text Society (original series).
Emden, *Cambridge*	Emden, A. B., *Biographical Register of the University of Cambridge to 1500* (Cambridge, 1963).
Emden, *Oxford*	Emden, A. B., *Biographical Register of the University of Oxford to 1500* (3 vols., Oxford, 1957–9).
Ferreres	Ferreres, J. B., *Historia del Misal Romano* (Barcelona, 1929).
Frere	Frere, W. H., *Bibliotheca Musico-Liturgica* (2 vols., Plainsong and Medieval Music Society, 1894–1932).
Grotefend, *Zeitrechnung*	Grotefend, H., *Zeitrechnung des Mittelalters und die Neuzeit* (2 vols., Hanover, 1891–8).
HBS	Henry Bradshaw Society.
Holweck, *Cal. Liturg.*	Holweck, F. G., *Calendarium Liturgicum* (Philadelphia, 1925).
Holyrood Ordinale	*Holyrood Ordinale*, ed. F. C. Eeles (Old Edinburgh Club vii, 1914).
Horae Ebor.	*Horae Eboracenses*, ed. C. Wordsworth (SS cxxxii, 1920).
Hourlier and du Moustier	Hourlier, J., and du Moustier, B., 'Le calendrier Cartusien', *Études grégoriennes* ii (1950), 151–61.
Janin	Janin, R., *La Géographie ecclésiastique de l'Église byzantin*, pt. i, vol. iii: *Les Églises et les monastères* (Paris, 1953).
Kallenberg	Kallenberg, P., *Fontes Liturgiae carmelitanae* (Rome, 1962).
Ker	Ker, N. R., *Medieval Libraries of Great Britain* (2nd edn., Royal Historical Society, 1964).
Kishpaugh	Kishpaugh, M. J., *The Feast of the Presentation in the Temple* (Washington, Catholic University of America dissertation, 1941).
Legenda Aurea	*Legenda Aurea*, ed. T. Graesse (2nd edn., Leipzig, 1850).
Leroquais, *Brevs.*	Leroquais, V., *Les Bréviaires manuscrits de bibliothèques publiques de France* (6 vols., Paris, 1934).

Leroquais, *Sacrs. & Miss.*	Leroquais, V., *Les Sacramentaires et missels manuscrits de bibliothèques publiques de France* (4 vols., Paris, 1924).
Mansi	Mansi, J. D., *Sacrorum Conciliorum Nova et Amplissima Collectio* (31 vols., Rome, 1758–98).
Missale Romanum 1474	*Missale Romanum 1474*, ed. R. Lippe (HBS xvii, 1899; xxiii, 1907).
Mon. Brev.	*Monastic Breviary of Hyde Abbey, Winchester*, ed. J. B. L. Tolhurst (HBS lxix, 1932; lxx, 1933; lxxi, 1934; lxxvi, 1938; lxxviii, 1939; lxxx, 1942).
PG	*Patrologia Graeca*, ed. J. P. Migne (162 vols., Paris, 1857–66).
PL	*Patrologia Latina*, ed. J. P. Migne (221 vols., Paris, 1844–64).
Records of Northern Conv.	*Records of the Northern Convocation*, ed. G. W. Kitchin (SS cxiii, 1907).
RH	Chevalier, U., *Repertorium Hymnologicum* (6 vols., Paris, 1892–1921).
de Riant	Riant, Comte de, *Exuviae Sacrae Constantinopolitanae* (2 vols., Geneva, 1877–8).
RS	Rolls Series.
SS	Surtees Society.
Test. Ebor.	*Testamenta Eboracensia*, ed. J. Raine and J. Raine, jnr. (SS iv, 1836; xxx, 1855; xlv, 1865; liii, 1869; lxxix, 1884).
VCH	*Victoria County History* (London, 1900–).
Westminster Missal	*Missale ad usum ecclesie Westmonasteriensis*, ed. J. W. Legg (HBS i, 1891; v, 1893; xii, 1897).
Wilkins	Wilkins, D., *Concilia Magnae Brittaniae et Hiberniae* (4 vols., London, 1737).
Wilmart, *Auteurs Spirituels*	Wilmart, A., *Auteurs spirituels et textes dévots du moyen âge latin* (Paris, 1932).
Wordsworth and Littlehales	Wordsworth, C., and Littlehales, H., *The Old Service Books of the English Church* (London, 1904).
Wormald i *or* ii	Wormald, F., *English Benedictine Kalendars after* A.D. *1100* (HBS lxxvii, 1939; lxxxi, 1946).
Wormald, *Eng. Kals. before 1100*	Wormald, F., *English kalendars before* A.D. *1100* (HBS lxxii, 1934).

PRINCIPAL MODERN EDITIONS OF MEDIEVAL ENGLISH SECULAR LITURGICAL TEXTS

(When cited in footnotes, citations are under short titles, as at left)

Sarum Missal: *Missale ad Usum Insignis et Praeclarae Ecclesiae Sarum*, ed. F. W. Dickinson (Burntisland, 1861–83). This is based on a collation of printed editions, and primarily on the 1526 Paris edition. The other modern edition of the Sarum Missal, by W. G. Legg (Oxford, 1916), is from three thirteenth- and fourteenth-century MSS.; it is consequently too early for our purposes, and Dickinson's edition is cited throughout.

Sarum Breviary: *Breviarum ad Usum Insignis Ecclesiae Sarum*, ed. F. Procter and C. Wordsworth (3 vols., Cambridge, 1879–86). Reproduces primarily the 1531 Paris edition. This is one of the three editions (1496, 1516, 1531) of the 'Great Breviary', which often contains longer lessons at matins than those of the 'Portiforium'. The complex arrangement of Procter and Wordsworth is sometimes baffling, but there are useful indices.

Sarum Gradual: *Graduale Sarisburiense*, ed. W. H. Frere (2 vols., Plainsong and Medieval Music Society, 1891–4). A facsimile of the earliest gradual of English origin known to exist, BM MS. Add. 12194 (mid thirteenth century).

Sarum Antiphoner: *Antiphonale Sarisburiense*, ed. W. H. Frere (3 vols., Plainsong and Medieval Music Society, 1901–25). A facsimile of, for the most part, the 'Barnwell Antiphoner', CUL MS. Mm. ii. 9 (mid thirteenth century), supplemented where necessary from other texts. Forms for the 'nova festa' are not supplied.

Sarum Processional: *Processionale ad Usum Insignis ac Praeclarae Ecclesiae Sarum*, ed. W. G. Henderson (Leeds, 1882). From the first edition, Rouen, 1508, collated with other editions and with three MSS.

Sarum Manual: *Manuale ad Usum Percelebris Ecclesie Sarisburensis*, ed. A. J. Collins (HBS xci, 1958). From the 1543 Rouen edition, compared with others.

Sarum Consuetudinary, Customary, Ordinal, Tonal: *The Use of Sarum*, ed. W. H. Frere (2 vols., Cambridge, 1898–1901). Most of the material in these volumes is taken from MSS. too early to be of use for our purposes.

York Missal: *Missale ad usum insignis ecclesiae Eboracensis*, ed. W. G. Henderson (SS lix, 1874; lx, 1874). A collation of the extant MSS. (fourteenth and fifteenth centuries) and of the five printed editions.

York Breviary: *Breviarium ad usum insignis ecclesiae Eboracensis*, ed. S. W. Lawley (SS lxxi, 1880; lxxv, 1883). Primarily a reprint of the first edition, Venice, 1493, with collations from MSS. and other editions. The indices have been subsumed in those of Procter and Wordsworth.

York Manual and Processional: *Manuale et processionale ad usum insignis ecclesiae Eboracensis*, ed. W. G. Henderson (SS lxiii, 1875).

Hereford Missal: *Missale ad Usum Percelebris Ecclesiae Herefordiensis*, ed. W. G. Henderson (Leeds, 1874). From the 1502 edition, collated with the fourteenth-century MS., Univ. Oxf. 78A.

Hereford Breviary: *The Hereford Breviary*, ed. W. H. Frere and L. E. G. Brown (HBS xxvi, 1904; xl, 1911; xlvi, 1915). From the Rouen edition of 1505, with collation of MSS. Excellent indices.

SCOTTISH

Arbuthnott Missal: *Liber Ecclesiae Beati Terrenani de Arbuthnott*, ed. A. P. and G. H. Forbes (Burntisland, 1864). From the manuscript of 1491.

Aberdeen Breviary: *Breviarium Aberdonense*, ed. W. J. Blew (2 vols., Bannatyne Club, 1854). (Separately printed introduction by D. Laing contains three supplementary offices, *c.* 1520.) A facsimile of Bishop Elphinstone's adaptation of a Sarum breviary for use in Scotland, 1510.

'Bute' Breviary: *Breviarium Bothanum*, ed. W. D. M(acray) (London, 1900). From a fifteenth-century MS. (formerly ?) owned by the Marquess of Bute, possibly for Dunkeld Cathedral.

DAYS IN THE LITURGICAL YEAR MOST FREQUENTLY REFERRED TO

Day	*New Feast*	*Principal older feast displaced*	*Roman name for date (martyrologies, kalendars, etc.)*
July 2nd	Visitation	Processus and Martinian (sometimes, Translation of Swithun)	vi Nones Julii
August 6th	Transfiguration	Sixtus, with Felicissimus and Agapitus	viii Idus Augusti
August 7th	Name of Jesus	Donatus	vii Idus Augusti
November 9th	'Iconia Domini'	Theodore	vi Idus Novembri
November 21st	Presentation	—	xi Kal. Decembri

I

INTRODUCTORY

THE primary evidence for our subject is that afforded by medieval service books: principally missals and breviaries (and their constituent parts when in separate volumes: graduals, legendaries, antiphoners, and the like), but also processionals, benedictionals, and the kalendars of psalters and of books of hours. A good deal of attention is to be paid to martyrologies, where awareness of a new observance is often first visible. But the appearance of a notice in, or added to, a martyrology must not be taken as indicating liturgical observance. Nor should the inclusion of a feast in a kalendar be necessarily so interpreted. All that can be said is that mentions in a kalendar or martyrology indicate some degree of recognition. These cautions are the more needed because it is necessary to argue a good deal from evidence of kalendars, since many more survive (especially in psalters), than of larger service books with full sets of variable forms. On the other hand, for our period inferences which might be drawn from ordinals must in general be discounted. Of all the books having to do with the performance of the liturgy the ordinal is probably the most conservative: because an ordinal (and its subsequent application in the 'pie') must have been a very great deal of trouble to work out—as indeed its purpose of regularizing and providing a guide to the immense complexities of medieval services indicates—and having once been worked out, it is unlikely that it would be altered each time a change was introduced. An ordinal is also in some sense an idealization, particularly since one of the succession of Salisbury ordinals was sooner or later adopted by the majority of great English churches about which we possess such information.[1] Changes in the original ordinal, extensive or minimal, were generally made,

[1] For English ordinals in general see Frere, *The Use of Sarum* ii (Cambridge, 1901).

but the impression remains that, whereas ordinals were originally meant to be practical guides to the celebration of the services, they became theoretical norms which a combination of innovation, laziness, and individualism rapidly made obsolete.

The inferences which could be drawn from ordinals would in any case be largely negative, since they were mostly compiled before the new feasts we are considering gained currency. This brings up the problem of negative evidence. In any field where only a small fraction of the original evidence survives, and that largely on the basis of chance, the value of the argument from silence is gravely limited. Yet, if we are to say anything at all about the subject, it is necessary to infer that, for example, because a mass for the Holy Name is not found in a missal of 1461 the feast was not at that time observed in the church for which the missal was written. Still, this kind of argument has to be admitted only with great caution.

Descriptions of liturgical manuscripts (such as those in the standard catalogues enumerated in the Preface) are of necessity based on a general view of such matters as handwriting, illumination, specific local indications like dedication feasts or inscriptions of ownership, and contents. The latter factor is in turn judged partly from a consensus of which feasts, with which forms, were used in which places at which time. Such judgements—for instance, that the presence of St. Anne, in the original hand, in an English kalendar indicates that it was written after 1383, when the feast was established in England in honour of the marriage of Richard II and Anne of Bohemia—are inescapable if one is to say anything about liturgical manuscripts at all; despite the fact that in this case several English kalendars which are indisputably earlier than that date contain the feast in the original hand.[1] The imprudence of relying entirely on commonly used dates of 'acceptance' is most clearly illustrated by the feast of the Transfiguration, which was officially promulgated by Callistus III in 1457. Now, no one seeing the Transfiguration in a kalendar, in a hand which looked like that of the early thirteenth century, and was

[1] H. M. Bannister stated that he had found St. Anne in nineteen kalendars of before 1383, more than half of them before 1340: *Liber Obituarius Aulae Reginae in Oxonia* (Oxford Historical Society lvi, 1910), xiii.

uniform with the rest of the text, and in which all other indications of date (e.g. the absence of Corpus Christi) pointed to the same period, would argue that the manuscript was written after 1457. But it might very conceivably be stated that a manuscript which was in fact written in, say, 1420, was post-1457 because it included the Transfiguration in its original text.

This is not a matter of great importance, provided one realizes that all ascriptions of dates to liturgical manuscripts (in the absence of precise dating by the scribe)[1] must be regarded as provisional, that there always exists the possibilty of revision of the ascribed dates in the light of new evidence, and that not a great deal has been known about precisely how a new feast was either promulgated—at all the levels needed to make it generally effective—or accepted. One of the principal aims of the present study is to try to shed some light on this problem.

It may be helpful to list briefly the 'milestones' by which later medieval English kalendars are sometimes dated.[2] The feast of St. Anne (July 26th), in 1383, has already been mentioned; in 1415 those of David (March 1st), Chad (March 2nd), and Winifred (November 3rd) were accepted by Convocation of Canterbury, and in 1416 that of John of Beverley (May 7th, Deposition; York province also observed Translation, October 25th). Osmund was canonized in 1456/7, and his cult found, naturally, quick acceptance throughout the Sarum use, with two feasts, the Deposition (December 4th) and Translation (July 16th) being celebrated. This feast of his Deposition was ordered by Convocation of Canterbury in 1480, along with those of Etheldreda (June 23rd), Frideswide (October 19th), and Visitation (July 2nd). Evidence about official acceptance of the

[1] Even such a windfall as this must not always be used incautiously. In the chapter on the Visitation it will be argued that one such precisely dated manuscript (Bodl. MS. Lat. liturg. f. 29) is in fact erroneously dated, by a scribal slip from '1483' to '1443'.

[2] Lists of the dates of 'introduction' of feasts can be found in Wordsworth and Littlehales, pp. 190–3, and in Frere's introduction to the *Sarum Gradual* ii, pp. xxv–xxvii. The principal source for such lists is Wilkins. (Unfortunately the current revision of Wilkins extends at present only to 1313.) These lists are bound to be misleading. They are based inevitably on official decrees, and present a picture of liturgical change as a series of 'faits accomplis' rather than as the process of germination, initial extension, and wider popularity which is more nearly the case. It must be stressed that many of the above feasts had been celebrated locally for a long time.

Transfiguration (August 6th) points to 1487 in the southern province, and the Name of Jesus (August 7th) was similarly established the next year. (These two feasts were established in the province of York in 1489, and the Visitation in 1513.)

This summary listing brings up two large problems. First, what exactly do we mean by the introduction of a feast? As we shall see, papal promulgation, even if it commanded observance of a feast throughout the church, was not sufficient, at any rate not in England. Provincial legislation was also generally needed, but even then observance was probably not 'universal' for a long time—partly because the mechanics of getting a new feast celebrated were somewhat complicated. A reliable text of the office and mass (or of *an* office and mass if, as was often the case, there were more than one) had to be obtained, copied as many times as would have been necessary, and inserted into whatever combination of service books was in use at the particular church. (In addition, there was always the possibility that the new feast would conflict with an established local feast, and consequent adjustments would have to be made.) Because so few medieval service books have survived, and because there is still much we do not—and probably cannot ever—know about the actual services (as opposed to the idealization of ordinals and 'pies'), we tend to think of liturgical change as being a much simpler matter than it can in fact have been. We cannot know, except inferentially from occasional inventories, how many service books any church, great or small, had in use at any one time, or, more important, what was in them all.[1] Take the case of a parish church served by one priest. A single missal would have sufficed, to which masses for new feasts could have been added relatively easily. The priest was also, in our period, theoretically bound to say the complete divine office daily, which would presumably mean the copying out of the often lengthy offices for new feasts and inserting them into whatever form of breviary he possessed. It is hardly conceivable that this should have been done in even as many cases as with the missals;

[1] By Ker's reckoning, there survive of the liturgical books of Christ Church, Canterbury—where even at the dissolution there were fifty-eight monks—one missal, one breviary, and perhaps ten psalters (of a kind which could be used for services); of Durham one breviary, one gradual, one sequentiary, and two psalters; of Glastonbury, *none*; of such a great secular establishment as St. Paul's, London, one psalter.

and the extensive use of votive masses (which could be said on any day except a 'double') and of commemorations (which interrupted the course of the office as frequently as three times a week) must have fairly thoroughly broken down the supposed daily correlation between mass and office. This correlation would have been more closely maintained in a larger monastic or collegiate church, but in these cases the problem of supplying a new text for all the many service books—antiphoners, legendaries, and collectars (or the massive choir breviaries); processionals, missals, graduals, and epistle- and gospel-books at the very least—would have been immense, unless there were a large and somewhat underemployed scriptorium.

'The introduction of a feast', then, cannot mean that each new feast established by authority was immediately observed in every church in the kingdom. Reformation, and counter-Reformation, ideas of liturgical uniformity simply do not fit for the middle ages. Nor can we reasonably think of liturgical change as always coming, as it were, from the top. Most feasts (even, apparently the Visitation, though the evidence seems scant here) are observed somewhere, often in many places, before being officially promulgated. There were, of course, feasts connected with monasteries, either international (the special solemnities of the founders and worthies of orders) or originally local (like, in England, the feasts of Alban or Cuthbert or Augustine of Canterbury). These tended early to be commemorated throughout the kingdom. But other local figures would have had for a long time only a regional or diocesan cult: for instance, Chad of Lichfield, David of Wales, John of Beverley, Erkenwald of London, Osmund of Salisbury, William of York, Richard of Chichester. Later these became 'synodal feasts', though it is hard to tell precisely in what sense this term is used. In general it seems to mean the same as 'provincial', but some dioceses had their own 'festa synodalia'.

Terms like 'provincial' and 'synodal' suggest the second large problem: what were the actual liturgical patterns of later medieval England? It is customary to think of 'uses' in this connection, and this is certainly a primary pattern; but the idea of a neat division among the three (or four or five) uses is probably more a consequence of Cranmer's famous preface to the Book of Common Prayer than an accurate reflection of the highly complex situation.[1] Besides uses, we must consider provinces, dioceses, religious orders, and religious houses, and the nature of certain geographical areas; and we must not forget the special liturgical role of cathedrals. A few brief instances will show how these units interacted. The Sarum use was predominant in the province of Canterbury; but in the same province the uses of Hereford, Lincoln, and St. Paul's are found. Of the dioceses which had secular cathedral chapters, Lincoln and London were the two greatest in the province, but neither use spread very far beyond the cathedral church involved, certainly not throughout the respective dioceses. Hereford use was more widespread throughout that diocese (and occasionally beyond), but Hereford was in a way the most remote diocese of the province, and its peculiarities seem to owe something to a combination of French influences and insularity. Sarum use, however, was followed not only in the southern province, but also in some parts of the diocese of York, and more widely in the diocese of Durham, where encroachment from York was always feared. York use, then, was neither provincial nor diocesan in extent, though widely employed throughout the north of England.

Within the religious orders, the degree of liturgical uniformity varied. The 'monastic rite' was generally followed by Benedictines as far as the office was concerned;[2] but a great Benedictine house was as susceptible of influences from the rites (perhaps a technically inaccurate word here, but 'use' tends to be misleading, for reasons we have just seen) around it, including feasts observed, as it was likely to influence its neighbourhood or even diocese. The Augustinians generally followed the customs of the diocese in which they were.[3] The characteristic rites of the Cistercians, Carthusians, and Premonstratensians remained more distinct than those of the numerically greater Benedictines

[1] For a miscellany of frequently encountered information about the complicated and unclear question of the English uses, consult (but with caution) A. A. King, *Liturgies of the Past* (London, 1959), 276–374. *York Missal* ii, pp. ix–xvi, prints the distinctive remains of Lincoln, 'Bangor', and 'St. Asaph's' uses. The existence of a Bangor use is highly doubtful, and of a St. Asaph's use extremely unlikely.

[2] The 'monastic rite' in general is copiously discussed in J. B. L. Tolhurst, *The Monastic Breviary of Hyde Abbey, Winchester* vi (Introduction to the English Monastic Breviaries; HBS lxxx, 1942).

[3] See introduction to *Holyrood Ordinale*, ed. F. C. Eeles (Old Edinburgh Club vii, 1914).

(including Cluniacs) and Augustinians.[1] The friars' liturgical customs did not have a great deal of effect on the English secular liturgies. Indeed, the Dominican and Carmelite rites were both probably influenced by the Sarum, and there may also possibly have been English influence on the Franciscan liturgy, which in turn strongly influenced the Roman. The fourth major order of friars, the Austins, used the Roman liturgy.[2]

To draw a map, or even a series of maps, of the liturgical divisions of later medieval England would be, then, a nearly three-dimensional undertaking. It would have to differentiate between two provinces, five or six 'uses', the great religious houses, and twenty-one dioceses. But it would also have to indicate, though in not very bold colours, some idea of the liturgical identity, or at least homogeneity, of certain geographical areas. For example, East Anglia (above the Stour; below it was the diocese of London) was a natural geographical unit centred on the cathedral city and church of Norwich. The diocese of Norwich, not unnaturally, becomes a distinct unit in the sense that, say, Winchester does not. There are distinctively 'Norwich' kalendars and Norwich 'festa synodalia'.[3] Another such area was the diocese of Exeter (covering Cornwall as well as Devon), as the unusually elaborate liturgical compositions and directions of Bishop Grandisson indicate.[4] To a lesser degree, the dioceses of Worcester and Lichfield tended also to have a distinct liturgical identity. The medieval diocese of Lincoln was perhaps too vast for this to be true, except in those parts—probably only the area around the cathedral city—which followed the Lincoln 'use'. What seems to emerge, though only

[1] A. A. King, *Liturgies of the Religious Orders* (London, 1955). This book and the same author's *Liturgies of the Past* (which contains a chapter on English medieval rites) are not always either accurate or clear, but they provide a convenient modern summary of information culled from older works.

[2] For the Dominicans, see W. R. Bonniwell, *A History of the Dominican Liturgy* (New York, 1944), for the Franciscans S. J. P. van Dijk and J. H. Walker, *Origins of the Modern Roman Liturgy* (London, 1960), and for the Carmelites, P. Kallenberg, *Fontes liturgiae carmelitanae* (Rome, 1962). For the Gilbertine canons, *The Gilbertine Rite* (HBS lix, 1921; lx, 1922). The English Bridgettines on the whole adapted the Sarum rite.

[3] The Norwich 'festa synodalia' (separately collected in, e.g., BM MS. Cott. Jul. B. vii and St. John's Cbg. MS. 270) were Felix, Edmund, Dominic, Thomas of Hereford, and Francis.

[4] Collected in *Ordinale Exon.* (HBS xxxvii, 1909; xxxviii, 1909; lxiii, 1926; lxxix, 1940).

tentatively, is a not surprising pattern of some individuality in the districts lying outside the south-east and south-central 'core' of England: liturgically, Salisbury, Winchester, Canterbury, and London (despite the separate 'St. Paul's' use).

This picture begins to be simplified before the end of the middle ages. The greatest influence in this direction—one which is incalculable in its extent—is the spread of printing. Manuscript service books are differentiated by 'use' only through approximation: a missal with distinctly Sarum features, even though it may possess a number of peculiar characteristics of its own and have been copied from a succession of books all having in turn their own characteristics, is still called a 'Sarum missal'. But with printing, *the* missal 'ad Usum Insignis et Praeclarae Ecclesiae Sarum', for example, came into being. Though, as we shall see, there were changes in the successive editions of printed service books, the degree of standardization which was possible was much greater. What one speaks of as a 'Sarum office',[1] though frequently to be found in manuscript books, is definitely established, so to speak, by its presence in the printed editions. So when, in the chapters to follow, the 'York mass' or 'Hereford office' is spoken of, it is with reference primarily to the forms found in the printed books (which in turn exist in modern, and for the most part reliable, editions). Precisely what manuscript text or texts the early printers worked from is a question which has so far, unfortunately, not been answered. We can generally assume that the texts they used were not notably unrepresentative.

A word needs to be added about the Scottish service books, to which reference is often made. Though Scotland was throughout our period a separate kingdom from England, the Sarum use was predominant there from roughly the thirteenth century. The number of surviving liturgical books is not great,[2] but there are two or three late ones of particular interest, and which are available in either modern or facsimile editions. The missal copied for the church of St. Terrenan, Arbuthnott, by J. Sib-

[1] Indeed, the Sarum use came to be so predominant in England at the end of the middle ages that it is frequently convenient to speak of the 'Sarum' mass or office when what is meant is that held in common by Sarum and York and, generally, Hereford.

[2] Some help in identifying what does survive is given in D. McRoberts, *Catalogue of Scottish Medieval Liturgical Books and Fragments* (Glasgow, 1953).

bald in 1491 is in most respects a Sarum missal, with some differences in the sanctorale. In the absence of a late medieval Scottish printed missal, the Arbuthnott missal (though a manuscript book) has been taken as typical of usage in Scotland at the period of the earliest printed service books. Such an assumption is not without risks, but there is, literally, no alternative. There is no 'matching' breviary, but one earlier and one later. Of these, the mid fifteenth-century breviary now called the *Breviarium Bothanum* (from its modern owner, the Marquess of Bute) was perhaps intended for Dunkeld and again follows Sarum use very closely, though some other influences are also present. In 1510 Bishop Elphinstone of Aberdeen, with royal encouragement, tried to begin codification of a national 'Scottish' use by issuing the printed *Breviarium Aberdonense*, based on a Sarum model but with considerable changes, especially in the sanctorale. An extra sheet of eight leaves, printed as a sort of supplement in about 1520, was inserted into the copy of the breviary at Glamis; this contains forms for the Compassion, the Crown of Thorns, and the Translation of the Relics of St. Andrew. These Scottish books are important for our investigation because it happens that among the principal variations from their Sarum models are different or unique forms for several of the feasts we are concerned with: for the Transfiguration and 'Iconia' in the Arbuthnott missal, for the 'Iconia' in the Aberdeen breviary (as well as for two of the feasts in the supplement, mentioned above), and for the Visitation in the Bute breviary.[1]

Continental service books sometimes offer germane comparisons. The catalogues of Ebner and Leroquais provide useful surveys of some principal manuscripts in Italy (for mass books only) and France respectively; while the work of Ferreres (also for mass books only) is similarly helpful for Spain; it is regrettable that there appears to be no similar survey for Germany. Not surprisingly, Scandinavian references appear several times; the influence of England on the Norwegian use of Trondheim (Nidaros) was considerable, but it is also true that some developments in the observance of our new feasts came sooner to Scandinavia than to England. It is, naturally, to Roman books

[1] In Ireland, too, the Sarum use was widespread, and we shall occasionally notice Irish service books.

that reference is most often made for purposes of comparison. The *editio princeps* of the Roman missal, Milan, 1474, has been published in a modern edition which includes collation with subsequent editions until the issue of the Pian missal in 1570. There is no modern edition of a pre-Pian (1568) Roman breviary; those of 1505 (Venice), 1520 (Paris), and 1534 (Venice) have been used.

Several times in the succeeding chapters we shall encounter the figure of John of Würzburg, a German pilgrim who visited the Holy Land probably between 1160 and 1170.[1] He was interested in liturgical matters, and his witness is invaluable for his inclusion of certain liturgical texts used at the church of the Holy Sepulchre. Both the Transfiguration and the Presentation seem to have been celebrated there in the mid twelfth century, with forms which later became common in the West but which at the time had little or no currency there. The Jerusalem (Latin) liturgy is generally, and confidently, stated to be French in origin.[2] But there were many diverse elements in the city during the Crusades—John himself enumerates some twenty-six 'nations'—and all sorts of liturgical influences would be present.

Another influence which will often be encountered is that of the *Legenda Aurea*. This work was compiled, generally from standard sources of the lives of saints to be found in legendaries, passionals, martyrologies, and the like, by Jacobo da Voragine in the mid thirteenth century. Its arrangement is more or less chronological, but centred on the story to be told rather than the date (as a martyrology would be), though supplementary happenings of the same day are sometimes added at the end of the stories. A number of additions were made after Jacobo's death, and among these are several which have an important bearing on the feasts we shall be considering. These accretions kept this always popular work up to date; the original one hundred and eighty-two chapters had grown by the time of the

[1] The least good of the principal manuscripts (Monac. 8458) was edited by Krinner and published by B. Pez in 1721, being subsequently reprinted by Migne in *PL* clv. 1053–88. A better edition, made from the Tegernsee MS. (Monac. 19418) was printed by Titus Tobler, *Descriptiones Terrae Sanctae* (Leipzig, 1874). Tobler's version is divided into twenty-seven chapters, of which chapter iv includes the forms for the Presentation missing from Krinner's version and hence from Migne's.

[2] e.g. F. Wormald in H. Buchthal, *Miniature Painting in the Latin Kingdom of Jerusalem* (Oxford, 1957), 107 ff.

early printed editions of about 1470, to two hundred and eighty, and in Caxton's translation to some four hundred and forty-eight![1] Unfortunately the standard modern edition of the work, by T. Graesse,[2] gives no help with the identification of the authors or dates of the supplementary chapters. In most of the cases in which we are interested the source can be figured out—a papal bull, or lessons from a breviary, or a chronicle—but this does not help us much in knowing to what extent inclusion in a supplementary chapter influenced liturgical acceptance of the feast connected with a particular story, and to what extent the process happened the other way round. An intensive study of the very large number of surviving manuscripts and early printed editions would be necessary before an answer could be even attempted.

Two things must be iterated: first, that what we are dealing with is a matter of gradual process, not of a series of steps, much less of overnight change. We can try to understand and describe the process only by isolating the stages of it at which there is definite evidence, but this procedural necessity must not mislead us into thinking of liturgical change as a cut-and-dried affair. The general pattern which may be established is that notice of a new feast would be most likely to appear first in a martyrology; then as an addition to the kalendar of a psalter or missal (which, as we said earlier, does not necessarily imply observance); then perhaps among the votives and supplementary masses of the missal (following the course which Henry Bradshaw described: 'It is very curious to see how the "nova festa" gradually worked their way into the text, first in an appendix, then a reference in the text saying that they would be found in full " in fine libri", then in full in their place . . .');[3] then, or concurrently, in the breviary, following the same course; then in the kalendar of books of hours, which, perhaps because they are not concerned with liturgical observances, tended to have sometimes the most sparse and/or conservative (i.e. outdated) kalendars, with the possible exception of feasts of the Virgin. Last of all the feast might be included in an ordinal or other directory, but this, as we have seen, is unlikely.

[1] J. Baudot, 'Jacques de Voragine', *DTC* viii (1924), 310–13.

[2] All references will be made to the second edition, Leipzig, 1850.

[3] *Sarum Breviary* iii, p. lii.

Secondly, it must be stressed that the fragmentary and haphazard nature of the evidence leaves this study open-ended. Though virtually all the available evidence has been used, the evidence which no longer exists might lead to different conclusions, in whole or in part, in several of these chapters. This point is worth making only because the evidence which no longer exists far outweighs the surviving remainder—a fact which is responsible for much of the fascination, as well as many of the difficulties, of the subject.

II

THE FEAST OF THE TRANSFIGURATION

THE most important fact about the feast of the Transfiguration is, for our purposes, its antiquity. The significance of its being regarded in fifteenth-century England as one of the 'nova festa' can be understood only in the light of the long and complex history which the feast had before then. It had been observed for centuries, in the West as well as in the East, by the time Callistus III officially promulgated it as a universal feast in 1457, ostensibly in thanksgiving for the defeat of the Turks at Belgrade the previous year. It has long been recognized that Callistus's 'institution' was really only an extension;[1] the origins of the feast can be traced back into the early middle ages, and even to patristic times. It is said that in the East Gregory the Illuminator (d. 390) originated the feast, or alternatively that the dedication in the fourth century of a church on Mt. Tabor, popularly supposed to be the site of the occurrence, was its initiating occasion,[2] rather like the feast of All Saints and the dedication of the Pantheon. In any event the feast appears early in Eastern service books.[3]

There is no clear evidence that the Western observance was directly borrowed from, or dependent on, the East, except probably in the matter of date. The Eastern feast seems always to have been observed around August 6th, but the earliest Western use for the story (as recorded in Matthew) is as the gospel for Ember Saturday in Lent. This was as early as the fifth century: Leo the Great preached an Ember-tide sermon on the text.[4] The expansion of the liturgical kalendar, and the

[1] e.g. Wadding, *Annales* ad an. 1456, no. lxviii (Rome, 1735; xii. 378).

[2] For the first explanation, G. Löw, *EC* xii. 439, citing the seventh-century Armenian bishop Gregory Asharuni; for the second, F. G. Holweck, *Cal. Liturg.* 258.

[3] K. Kellner, *Heortologie* (2nd edn., Freiburg i. B., 1906), 80; V. Grumel, 'Sur l'ancienneté de la fête de la Transfiguration', *Revue des études byzantines* xiv (1956), 209–10.

[4] *Sermo* LI, alias XCIV: *PL* liv. 308. Matt. 7 : 1–9 was appointed for Ember

tendency to transfer commemorations falling in Lent to another time[1] may have coincided with knowledge of the Eastern feast to bring about awareness of a possible observance in late July or early August.[2] Two mentions of such an awareness in eighth- and ninth-century Spain are sometimes cited as proving Mozarabic observance of the Transfiguration, but neither can be regarded as conclusive. The first is a letter of the year 764 written to an otherwise unknown bishop Felix of Cordova, in which the Transfiguration is referred to as preceding the September fast, but in such obscure language as to make it impossible to tell whether an actual liturgical observance is meant.[3] The second is a treatise on the eucharistic bread, dated internally at the year 845, in which an otherwise unknown Spanish bishop, Eldefonsus (Ildefonsus), ascribes to the feast, which he dates July 27th, the dignity of three masses, as at Christmas and Easter. But in this case the lack of any other information about the writer makes it by no means certain that he is talking about the Mozarabic rite.[4]

In fact, genuine Mozarabic liturgical documents are unanimous in not including the Transfiguration.[5] It is only in kalendars and sanctorales of the eleventh century, as the Mozarabic rite is being first heavily influenced and then supplanted by the ('Hispano'-)Roman, that the feast appears. The earliest

Saturday in Lent in both the 'standard' gospel series (end of eighth century) and the 'earlier' series (mid eighth century), as given in W. H. Frere, *Studies in Early Roman Liturgy* ii (Alc. xxx, 1934), § 67.

[1] The same process took place in the case of the Visitation, which would fall more in accord with the biblical chronology shortly after the Annunciation than nine days after the birth of John the Baptist; and it is interesting that in the York use, where the feast was not accepted until the late date of 1513, logic took precedence over liturgical convenience, and April 2nd was the appointed day. See next chapter.

[2] Both the kalendar of St. Willibrord (first decade of the eighth century) and the martyrology of Oengus (*c.* 800) include the Transfiguration towards the end of July, on the 27th and 26th respectively (HBS lv (1918), 9; HBS xxix (1905), 165); the martyrology of Wandelbert, a monk of Prüm writing in the first half of the ninth century, mentions the Transfiguration at the beginning of the entry for August 6th (*PL* cxxi. 607).

[3] G. Morin, 'Un évêque de Cordove inconnu et deux opuscules inédits de l'an 764', *Revue bén.* xv (1898), 290.

[4] *PL* cvi. 886.

[5] The Mozarabic observance referred to by some commentators, e.g. Bäumer i. 428, in the *Missale mixtum secundum regulam Beati Isidorii* (*PL* lxxxv. 806), is of course much later than Isidore's time, being an edition compiled at the instigation of Cardinal Ximenes.

Spanish service forms we have for it, those of the Vich sacramentary of 1038 (mass prayer and a preface for vigil as well as feast with an alternative post-communion for the feast), are related to others known to have been used in Italy earlier.[1]

In some south Italian fragments found at Peterling (Payerne) in Switzerland, written in about the year 1000 in a 'Beneventan' hand (perhaps from Bari), the forms for most of a mass of the Transfiguration are preserved.[2] The fragment begins in mid-epistle, and is complete thereafter. There are three important things about it. First, the lessons, Phil. 3 : 19–4 : 1 (probably from 3 : 17 originally) and Luke 9 : 26 ff., are not otherwise known as lessons for the Transfiguration. The passage from Philippians seems normally to have been used sometime during the late summer in the early Roman lectionaries,[3] the passage from Luke not at all.[4] This epistle is rather subtly appropriate to the Transfiguration story, and may, as we shall see, have had some influence on all later offices for the feast. There was certainly an Old Testament reading also, but this is now missing. Secondly, the last three of the mass chants are preserved, thus forming the oldest extant chants for the feast: an alleluia, 'Dominus regnavit', an offertory, 'Deus enim firmavit', and a communio, 'Revelabitur gloria domini'. Of these, the alleluia and offertory pass into some of the later masses, including the Sarum. Finally, the secret and post-communion (the collect is lacking) are identical with the corresponding prayers in the Vich sacramentary for the *vigil* of the feast. The same is true of the preface.

The Vich and Peterling texts witness, then, to at least an

[1] Ed. Alejandro Olivar, *El Sacramentario de Vich* (Monumenta Hispaniae Sacra, serie liturgica iv; Madrid–Barcelona, 1953), 74–5. This sacramentary has been discussed by J. B. Ferreres in his *Historia del Misal Romano* (Barcelona, 1929), 333 ff., which contains the fullest treatment of the Transfiguration to be found in any modern work; and also, almost identically, in his article 'La Transfiguration de Notre Seigneur. Histoire de sa fête et de sa messe', *Ephemerides Theologicae Lovanienses* v (1928), 630–43.

[2] Ed. Alban Dold, *Die Züricher und Peterlingen Messbuch Fragmente* (Texte und Arbeiten i. 25; Beuron, 1934), 25–6. Dold suggests that observance of the Transfiguration originated under Greek influence, in southern Italy (p. lxx).

[3] Frere, *Studies* . . . iii (Alc. xxxii, 1935), 18, 43.

[4] Tenth- and eleventh-century Monte Cassino instances have been noted which use the Markan account for the Gospel: S. Beissel, *Entstehung der Perikopen des römischen Messbuches* (Freiburg i. B., 1907), 156. No information concerning the other mass forms is given.

incipient observance of the feast, and this is corroborated by evidence from elsewhere. In a manuscript from the monastery of Valcassoriana in Umbria containing an epistle-book of the tenth century, the lesson for the Transfiguration is 2 Pet. 1 : 15–19, the normal Western epistle (though there is some variation in the number of verses). There is also an Old Testament lesson, Ecclus. 24 : 1–5, 21–22; and an epistle for the vigil, Rev. 1 : 13–18.[1] Another (supposedly) tenth-century example is in an addition to a ninth-century Tours sacramentary composed of fragments.[2] Both Leroquais and Ebner cite several eleventh-century mentions of the feast from France and Italy, and a larger number from the twelfth century.[3]

In the twelfth century, indeed, the feast seems to have been becoming widespread. John of Würzburg, in his description of the Holy Land in the middle of the twelfth century, gives some forms for a mass of the Transfiguration used at the church of the Holy Sepulchre.[4] The prayers are identical with those for the feast in the Vich sacramentary; and the chants (no lessons are given) are dealt with in an omnibus rubric at the beginning: 'Introitus, et missa per totum: Benedicta sit sancta, etc.', that is, the mass of the Trinity (or for Trinity Sunday, if that feast was observed in Jerusalem then). The connection between the two commemorations is the more likely because of the Trinitarian implications of the gospel story, the voice from the cloud suggesting a parallel to the voice and accompanying dove at the baptism of Christ.[5]

The link between these earliest observances of the Trans-

[1] Frere, *Studies* . . . iii. 69.

[2] Leroquais, *Sacrs. & Miss.* i. 51.

[3] Ibid. i. 153, 159, 168, 172(?), 185 (two of these have vigils also); Ebner, 5, 14, 19, 34, 65, 196, 221.

[4] *PL* clv. 1090. Earlier (col. 1057), John has mentioned Mt. Tabor as the site of the Transfiguration, in commemoration of which a feast is solemnly celebrated at Jerusalem; the text edited by T. Tobler (*Descriptiones Terrae Sanctae* (Leipzig, 1874), 112) adds the phrase 'in die sancti Sixti (i.e. August 6th) et maxime a surianis'. There is no way of telling exactly what John means by 'Syrians'. P. Radó, *Enchiridion Liturgicum* ii (Rome, 1961), 1304, suggests that the feast was known in the Holy Land at least by the time of Pope Sylvester II (999–1003), who himself accorded it some degree of recognition. Radó gives no authority for these statements, which have not been encountered elsewhere; it is striking, however, that Sylvester (Gerbert of Reims) was educated near Vich.

[5] The same connection can be seen in a thirteenth- and fourteenth-century breviary of the Teutonic knights, cited in Leroquais, *Brévs.* ii. 154: 'omnia sicut in festo Trinitatis'. Again, in Ximenes's appendix (late fifteenth or early sixteenth century) to the Mozarabic 'Breviarium Gothicum', to which we have already

figuration and its recognition in England seems to be Peter the Venerable (d. 1156). Though it is possible that knowledge of the feast may have passed direct from, say, Spain, this seems less likely than that the strong emphasis which the great Cluniac abbot gave to the observance influenced its introduction into England. During Peter's tenure as abbot the feast was made obligatory for all Cluniac houses: in 1132 it was decreed that 'Transfiguratio Domini eo more quo Purificatio sanctae mariae, excepta processione, cum lectionibus, responsoriis, et officiis ad diem pertinentibus, celebretur.'[1] This is especially interesting in that it appears to have been Peter himself who wrote the antiphons and responds on which the office in the English books was based. The office which Peter compiled[2] uses a sermon of his own,[3] as well as Leo's sermon, for the lessons. Though as we have seen, a mass of the Transfiguration existed by at least the beginning of the eleventh century,[4] no office is known earlier than Peter's in the mid twelfth century. It is worth while looking at this office in some detail.

Two hymns are specified: 'O nata lux' at first and second vespers and lauds, and 'O sator rerum' at matins. These hymns, which can be traced back to the tenth century, are virtually always found in manuscripts together, and provide a good deal

referred, the Transfiguration is marked 'Ut in die Sanctae Trinitatis' (*PL* lxxxvi. 1339).

1 M. Marrier, ed., *Bibliotheca Cluniacensis* (Paris, 1614), 1356. Here we have a different feast, that of the Purification, providing a model for the new observance of the Transfiguration.

2 Printed in Jean Leclercq, *Pierre le vénérable* (St. Wandrille, 1946), 379–90. The office is ascribed to Peter in a twelfth-century Cluniac lectionary, Paris BN MS. lat. 17716, f. 8 sqq., along with his statutes.

3 Marrier, ed., op. cit. 1231–48; reprinted in *PL* clxxxix. 953–72. It may seem strange and even doubtful that Peter would include selections from his own sermons as lessons for an office he was composing. But if this did not happen during his lifetime, it did so shortly thereafter, for Giles Constable has shown that Peter's sermons were being used as Cluniac lessons before the end of the twelfth century: 'Manuscripts of works by Peter the Venerable', *Pertus Venerabilis* (Studia Anselmiana xl; Rome, 1956), 238–40.

4 Although in both the Peterling and Vich texts the Transfiguration seems to be in its appropriate place in the sanctorale (in so far as one can tell from the fragmentary nature of the Peterling text) there are instances where the mass appears as an addition to the original text, among votives but not, most likely, as a votive: see Leroquais, *Sacrs. & Miss.* i. 201, ii. 93, 117. It is doubtful whether the Transfiguration ever had, like the Name of Jesus, an originally non-temporal commemoration, but a place in the divine office cannot necessarily be inferred from its inclusion in a missal or sacramentary.

of additional information about the early observance of the Transfiguration. They seem to appear first in Benedictine hymnaries of the tenth and eleventh centuries, principally from south central Italy (Benevento, Monte Cassino, Farfa, Naples), but also (perhaps the oldest) from Moissac in south-west France.[1] 'O sator rerum' contains nine stanzas in its earlier form; a shortened form of the first four and the ninth stanzas became common later, and is the version found in the English books.

Peter's office begins with the responsory after the capitulum of first vespers, and the other parts which are given specifically for that hour are the hymn, the versicle and response which follow it, and the antiphon to the Magnificat. The capitula are particularly interesting. Those at sext and none are, respectively. 2 Pet. 1 : 16–17 and 18–19, comprising, in the usual way, the standard epistle for the feast. But that for lauds (repeated at terce and vespers) is Phil. 3 : 20–21, which we saw was the beginning of the epistle in the Peterling fragment. Since the monastery at Peterling was also a Cluniac house (from 962), not a great distance from Cluny itself, it is not extravagant to speculate that Peter may have known the mass of the Transfiguration contained in that text.[2] In accordance with monastic practice for greater feasts, the office is of twelve lessons, the first eight from Peter's sermon, the last four from Leo's. Peter's antiphons and responds are, as Dom Jean Leclercq points out, largely biblical in tone.[3] Three different collects are specified in the office: 'Deus qui nos superno transfigurati' at lauds, 'Concede nobis Domine ad contuendam' at sext, and 'Fac nos quaesumus

[1] 'O nata lux': *RH* nos. 13297/8; 'O sator rerum': *RH* no. 13715; both are given in *AHMA* ii. 57 and li. 106–7, and 'O sator rerum' in xxiii. 18. Most of these early MSS. listed in *AHMA* are described conveniently in J. Mearns, *Early Latin Hymnaries* (Cambridge, 1913), which includes the two hymns. The MS. evidence of these hymnaries suggests an early Italian Benedictine observance of the feast: in Casinen. MS. 506, a tenth-century hymnary from Monte Cassino, the two hymns appear in the sanctorale about the sixth of August, and this is also the case in the Neapolitan hymnal of *c.* 1000, Vat. MS. lat. 7172 and Paris BN MS. lat. 1092. Moissac was a Cluniac house from 1052; it had been restored in the ninth century after being destroyed by the Saracens.

[2] It is possible that the 'Peterling missal' was brought there by 1061: Dold, op. cit., p. xvi. There is a strong likelihood that the Transfiguration was prominently recognized by the Cluniacs before the abbacy of Peter the Venerable. Two eleventh-century Cluniac service books containing the Transfiguration have been noticed by G. de Valous, who has collected a number of continental Cluniac kalendars: *La Monachisme clunisien des origines au xve siècle* i (Paris, 1935), 405.

[3] Op. cit. 381.

Domine' at none. A fourth collect is given as well, but this is rather part of the mass which follows, without identifying rubric, at the end of the office. After the hymn and antiphon to the Magnificat at second vespers, there are the words 'Ave stella matutina peccatorum', an antiphon of the Virgin the relevance of which to the matter at hand is not clear; then follow the lessons for the three nocturns; and then the mass, beginning with the collect 'Deus qui hodierna die'. The collect, secret, and post-communion here are identical with those in the Vich sacramentary for the feast (not for the vigil, like the Peterling fragment), as is the Vich alternative post-communion with Peter's collect at none. The prefaces, however, differ: the Cluniac is an adaptation—'transfigurati' replacing 'incarnati'—of the ancient Christmas preface 'Quia per incarnati verbi', and there is a similar adaptation in the 'Communicantes' section of the canon 'Memoriam celebrantes transfigurationis Domini'. Two chants are given: a gradual with alleluia, and a communio, neither like those in the Peterling fragment, but both identical with the (later) Sarum.

After these mass forms comes a curious collection of texts. First the capitulum from Philippians, then a repetition of the collect at lauds; and then the first of several farsed chants,[1] the Kyrie 'Te Christe supplices exoramus'. This is followed by another Kyrie, 'Clemens rector aeterne pater'. Then comes a sequence specifically about the Transfiguration, 'Fulget mundo celebris'. This is the earliest known appearance of this sequence,[2] which we shall see recurring in the English manuscripts. Next comes a farsed Sanctus, 'Ab aeterno disponens omnia solus', and another Kyrie, the widely-used 'Kyrie fons bonitatis', which Dom Jean Leclercq thinks may have been composed by Peter himself. Then there is another Sanctus, 'Perpetuo cuncta numine regens', and two farsed Agnus Dei's. The section concludes with the gospel from Matthew (17 : 1-9), and the words 'Credo in unum deum'. The manuscript then continues with a collection of Cluniac regulations. It is clear that these divers texts are meant to have some connection with the observance

[1] Most of these farsed chants were in common use; they may, for instance, be found in the 'Winchester Troper' (HBS viii, 1894), written in the late tenth and early eleventh centuries.

[2] *AHMA* liii. 149: the editors thought its origin was probably French.

of the Transfiguration, though only in the case of the sequence is the connection obvious.

It would be expected that English Cluniac houses would, following the legislation of 1132, observe the Transfiguration without exception, and this, from the small amount of evidence which we possess, appears to be the case. A Cluniac breviary of the early fourteenth century (1299–1315) from Pontefract[1] has the Transfiguration in blue in the kalendar, with an office of twelve lessons. This is largely Peter the Venerable's office, but the variations are noteworthy. The principal changes are in the response and versicle after the third lesson, where the responsory after the capitulum at lauds in Peter's office replaces the repetition of the responsory after the capitulum at vespers, 'Assumens Jesus'. The Pontefract responsory at lauds is then altered to 'Benedictus . . . / Et benedictum'. A new hymn is introduced at lauds, in place of 'O nata lux' a second time: 'Deus manens primordium'.[2] The collects are somewhat different: 'Deus qui hodierna die' (Peter's mass collect) is specified for first vespers, and also for lauds (replacing 'Deus qui nos superno transfigurati'), terce and second vespers. The capitula at the little hours are changed, 2 Pet. 1 : 18–19 now serving at sext instead of none, with 'Ut testimonium' at none being rather a paraphrase of scriptural words than a literal Bible verse. The lessons constitute the most important change. In place of the lessons taken from Peter's sermon, in the first two nocturns there is a division, into eight extremely brief lessons, of Jerome's commentary on Matt. 16 : 27–8[3] (the two verses which precede the Transfiguration story); and excerpts from Leo's sermon in the third nocturn are replaced by a selection from Bede's homily for the second Sunday in Lent[4]—as we have seen, the season when the Transfiguration story was read in the early Roman liturgy—on the story as it is found in St. Mark. Mark's account is given after lesson xii in the Pontefract breviary, which is again a difference from Peter the Venerable's office, based on St. Matthew's version.

[1] Univ. Oxf. MS. 101, f. 301.

[2] This is the earliest appearance of this hymn (*RH* no. 4457; *AHMA* iv. 20) which has been noticed. It also appears in an Italian Benedictine diurnal of the mid fifteenth century, Bodl. MS. Canon Liturg. 224, f. 260, along with 'O nata lux' and 'O sator rerum'.

[3] *In Matt.*, lib. III, cap. xvi: *PL* xxvi. 121.

[4] *Hom.* XVII: *PL* xciv. 96.

Another Pontefract book, a missal of the fifteenth century,[1] includes the Transfiguration in red in its kalendar and a mass (f. 134ᵛ) which is virtually identical with that given at the end of Peter's office. The two chants which are lacking in the manuscript containing Peter's office and mass are supplied: an introit 'In excelso throno . . . / Jubilate . . .', as for the Sunday after the octave of Epiphany; and an offertory, 'Deus enim firmavit', as in the Peterling fragment.

There are two other early Cluniac texts from English houses which should be noted. The first is the 'Bromholm Psalter', written for the Cluniacs at Bromholm in Norfolk.[2] In its kalendar, which is of the early fourteenth century, the Transfiguration is listed in red, and was, like other specially important feasts, to have been distinguished by a more elaborate initial, but the initials were never executed. In the second half of the psalter is a hymnal of the later fourteenth century which contains hymns for a small number of selected feasts. Among these are the two hymns from Peter's office, 'O nata lux', and 'O sator rerum' (f. 248); evidently the use of 'Deus manens primordium' for a third hymn, as in the Pontefract breviary, had not spread to Bromholm. The second document is a breviary, with missal offices, from the premier Cluniac priory in England, Lewes.[3] This, roughly contemporary with the Pontefract book, was written at various dates between 1262 and 1315. The sanctorale, which is the oldest of what seem to be three stages in the composition of the manuscript, contains an office of the Transfiguration (f. 386) which is again based on Peter's. In general it accords with the Pontefract version. The principal variations are in the hymns: 'O nata lux' is used at matins rather than vespers, 'O sator rerum' at lauds rather than matins, and a new hymn is introduced at vespers, 'Caelestis formam gloriae'. This hymn, as we shall see, becomes standard in the English secular office.[4] After the office come the mass forms, which agree with those in the Pontefract missal, but there is a proper preface:

[1] King's Cbg. MS. 31.

[2] Bodl. MS. Ashmole 1523.

[3] Fitzwilliam Mus. Cbg. MS. 369, formerly owned by G. Moreau. Discussion with some facsimiles in V. Leroquais, *Le Bréviaire-Missel du Prieuré Clunisien de Lewes* (Paris, 1935).

[4] Its appearance here is earlier than those noticed in *AHMA* lii. 16–17, which are from fourteenth-century French MSS. There it is generally found with the hymns 'Splendor aeterni luminis' and 'Celebri gaudio'.

'Qui hodierna die inter moysen et helyam transfiguratus tribus discipulis . . .'. The feast is gold in the kalendar, which is later than the sanctorale.

It is plain, then, that the Cluniac observance of the Transfiguration in England was based on the mass and office which Peter the Venerable had compiled. No English Cluniac evidence exists before 1262 at the earliest,[1] but we know the feast was celebrated in some (non-Cluniac) English Benedictine houses before then. In fact, the clearest example of an early observance of the Transfiguration in England is provided by St. Albans. Enough of its liturgical documents have survived to show us something of the process by which a new feast was assimilated into the worship of a great religious house, and to provide us with a sufficiently precise dating. Before 1170 the feast was not observed there;[2] by at least the beginning of the thirteenth century it was, as shown by a St. Albans sacramentary written early in the third quarter of the twelfth century, with additions extending up until about 1220.[3] In the margin of the sanctorale for August 6th (f. 95; St. Sixtus et al.) is added 'Eodem die Transfiguratio domini. Require in fine libri'. At the end of the original text (f. 158) are added masses of St. Amphibalus and the Transfiguration, followed by (in a slightly later hand?) the Nativity of St. Thomas of Canterbury. Of the set of prayers given for the Transfiguration, the secret and post-communion correspond to the prayers used by Peter the Venerable, but the collect, 'Deus qui hanc sacratissimam diem', is different. This peculiarity is also a feature of the mass for the feast in a St. Albans missal of 1308–26.[4] Here the Transfiguration is in red in the kalendar with the feast in its proper place in the sanctorale (f. 189). A full set of mass forms is given, corresponding in

[1] Perhaps the earliest English monastic notice is in the twelfth century (post-1121) Reading martyrology, BM MS. Harl. 82, where the entry for August 6th begins 'in monte thabor transfiguratio domini nostri jesu christi'. Though a Benedictine abbey, Reading was strongly influenced by Cluniac customs, and its first abbots were from Lewes: D. Knowles and R. N. Hadcock, *Medieval Religious Houses: England and Wales* (London, 1953), 74.

[2] As shown by four St. Albans kalendars of the twelfth century, BM MS. Roy. 2. A. x, BM MS. Eg. 3721, Mr. B. S. Cron's Psalter at Kew (formerly belonging to Sir Sidney Cockerell), and the Hildesheim Psalter: see O. Pächt et al., *The St. Albans Psalter* (London, 1960), 40. Cf. also Bodl. MS. Auct. D. 2. 6, the kalendar of which is probably from St. Albans.

[3] Bodl. MS. Rawl. liturg. c. 1.

[4] Bodl. MS. Laud misc. 279 (kalendar collated in Wormald i. 31–45).

every way (except for the collect) with those of Peter's mass as expanded in the Pontefract missal. Kalendars of 1235–60 show that by at least the second half of the thirteenth century the feast was of an important grade, 'in cappis', at the abbey.[1] It seems to have retained its importance right up to the time it was papally promulgated, for in 1430 a former precentor had built and the bishop of 'Chester' (Lichfield) consecrated, a new altar at St. Albans in honour of the Transfiguration and the Visitation.[2] Recognition of the feast passed to cells of St. Albans as well: kalendars of both Tynemouth[3] and Wymondham[4] (the latter 'in cappis'), in the first half of the fifteenth century, include the feast; and a Belvoir martyrology of the late thirteenth or early fourteenth century has the Transfiguration at the beginning of the entry for August 6th.[5]

Though an early observance can be found in some other Benedictine houses as well, it was by no means common. The two great houses of Canterbury, for instance, seem scarcely to have noticed the feast. The principal evidence for any recognition whatsoever is contained in an early thirteenth-century psalter[6] which has been ascribed to both Christ Church (by Frere and Ker) and St. Augustine's (by Wormald and Gasquet-Bishop). In the kalendar the Transfiguration has been included in red, by the original scribe, but set over to the right side of the column like the seasonal indications—the only feast in the entire kalendar to be treated in this manner. In the second half of the psalter is a hymnal, added by a later hand, which does not include the Transfiguration. A part from this psalter, the

[1] BM MS. Roy. 2. B. vi; New Coll. Oxf. MS. 358. Other thirteenth-century kalendars which contain the feast are BM MSS. Roy. 14. C. vii and Cott. Claud. D. vi, and Corpus Christi Cbg. MS. 26 (information on the latter kindly communicated to me by the Librarian, Dr. Richard Vaughan). BM MS. Cott. Jul. D. vii (mid thirteenth century) does not have the Transfiguration, but F. A. Gasquet and E. Bishop suggest (*The Bosworth Psalter* (London, 1908), 172) that there are St. Augustine's, Canterbury, elements in the kalendar (see below, n. 6).

[2] 'Chronicon Rerum Gestarum in Monasterio Sancti Albani' in *Amundesham Annales*, RS xxviii/5a (1870), 50. This altar will be discussed at greater length in the chapter on the Visitation.

[3] Bodl. MS. Gough liturg. 18 (kalendar collated in Wormald i. 31–45, as being St. Albans).

[4] Bodl. MS. Lat. liturg. g. 8.

[5] Trin. Cbg. MS. 1437 (O. 9. 25).

[6] Bodl. MS. Ashmole 1525. Wormald (i. 63–79) lists several of the principal kalendars for both these houses, and those for Christ Church are collated in Gasquet and Bishop, op. cit. 68–126.

feast does not seem to have appeared in kalendars of either house. Nor is it included in pre fifteenth-century books of such other great houses as Durham, Ely, Hyde, Norwich, Westminster, or Winchester.

There is no discernible factor common to those houses which did keep the feast before its general extension. An Evesham breviary of the third quarter of the thirteenth century includes the Transfiguration in its kalendar, in red;[1] but since only the winter half survives, no office is extant. The Worcester 'Portiforium Oswaldi' of the eleventh century has added to it three hymns for the Transfiguration—the two from Peter's office and 'Caelestis formam' as in the Lewes breviary—in a thirteenth- or fourteenth-century hand.[2] At York (St. Mary's abbey) a kalendar of about 1400 lists the feast in red.[3]

Among the Benedictine nuns, those of Amesbury seem to have observed it very early: it appears in blue (indicating a high grade) in the kalendar of a psalter of about 1220,[4] and in the kalendar of a book of hours of the next century.[5] If the attribution of the processional, of which only a nineteenth-century transcript at Solesmes is now extant, to the nuns of Wilton be correct, they were using chants taken from Peter the Venerable's office in probably the second half of the thirteenth century.[6] But the feast is not included in a rather earlier Wilton

[1] Bodl. MS. Barlow 41: printed in Wormald (ii. 21–38) where the date given—third quarter of the 'fourteenth century'—is almost certainly a misprint for 'thirteenth century'. Two Evesham kalendars collated by Wormald (BM MS. Lansdowne 427 of the mid thirteenth century and a loan to the BM of the first half of the fourteenth century) also contain the Transfiguration. The dating of Lansdowne 427 cannot be certain, since it is a copy of a manuscript badly burned by fire, and there is no way of telling which feasts were in the original hand and which have been added. Wormald cites BM MS. Cott. Vesp. B. xxiv, a twelfth-century Evesham 'caritates' list, as evidence for the very early observance of the feast there; but the list of feasts (f. 3) on which the Transfiguration appears between Mary Magdalen and the Assumption is on parchment of a different kind and in a later hand (probably fifteenth-century).

[2] Corpus Christi Cbg. MS. 391, f. 293. In James's catalogue, p. 243, the additional hand is called thirteenth-century; in a description of the MS. by Frere in Wordsworth and Littlebales, 75, perhaps fourteenth-century.

[3] Bod. MS. Lat. liturg. g. 1. This seems to be the only surviving liturgical document of this abbey.

[4] Bodl. MS. Liturg. 407. This was, however, in the period (1177–1403) during which the Amesbury nuns were of the order of Fontrevault.

[5] CUL MS. Ee. vi. 16.

[6] G. Benoit-Castelli, 'Un Processional Anglais du XIVème Siècle', *Ephemerides Liturgicae* lxxv (1961), 318.

kalendar of *c.* 1220–52.[1] The Transfiguration appears, in the original hand, in the kalendar of a Shaftesbury psalter of the twelfth century;[2] but this may not be as original as it seems, for, according to Boase, the illuminations show strong St. Albans influence.[3] In another celebrated psalter (St. Swithin's) which came to Shaftesbury from Winchester, the Transfiguration has been added to the kalendar in red in a later (fourteenth century?) hand.[4]

The so-called 'Barking Ordinal' of 1394–1404[5] shows in some detail the observance of the Transfiguration in a Benedictine nunnery in the period just before the feast was generally extended. In the Barking kalendar the feast is in red, and marked 'duplex' in the sanctorale. The office, for which only incipits are indicated, is marked by a distinctive collect at vespers, 'Deus qui nos sacrum transfigurationis', and by a third hymn (over Peter the Venerable's two) at lauds: 'Deus manens primordium', as in the Pontefract breviary. The lessons begin as do those in the Pontefract book, 'Petrus ad praedicationem'—Jerome's commentary on Matt. 16—but since the incipit only of the first lesson was given it is impossible to say what their extent was. Reference is made to the antiphoner, which is no longer extant, for the antiphons and responses. Incipits for procession and mass (not including prayers) follow those for terce; the chants of the mass, except for the alleluia, are as those in the St. Albans and Pontefract missals. The versicle at the alleluia is given simply as 'Ymera', with a reference to the feast of the Circumcision, which was one of four occasions during the year—with Christmas, Epiphany, and the Transfiguration—on which a special alleluia beginning with the Greek words '(H)ēmera (h)agios' was sung by the Barking nuns. The sequence indicated is 'Fulget mundo celebris', which was among the chants at the end of Peter the Venerable's mass.

[1] Royal College of Physicians MS. 409: see E. G. Millar, 'Les manuscrits à peintures des bibliothèques de Londres', *Bulletin de la Société Française de reproductions des manuscrits à peintures* (4th year, 1914–20), 132.

[2] BM MS. Lansdowne 383.

[3] T. S. R. Boase, *English Art 1100–1216* (Oxford, 1953), 108.

[4] BM MS. Cott. Nero C. iv; Boase, op. cit. 172–3.

[5] Univ. Oxf. MS. 169, printed HBS lxv–lxvi; the office of the Transfiguration is on p. 334 of the sanctorale. In another Barking kalendar of the same period (end of the fourteenth century) the Transfiguration is the first entry for August 6th, and in red; BM MS. Cott. Otho A. v.

Observance of the Transfiguration was even more sporadic among the Augustinians than among the Benedictines. But a few instances of Augustinian practice contribute materially to the picture of how awareness of this feast became general in England. Martyrologies, as has been said, tend to include mentions of feasts before (if ever) they are observed; in the case of an Augustinian martyrology from St. Osyth's in Essex, written in the third quarter of the twelfth century,[1] the interval between a notice of the feast and its observance is relatively brief. At the end of the entry for August 6th, we find, in the original hand, 'Eodem die Transfiguratio domini nostri Jesu Christi in monte excelso'. The feast was not originally included in the kalendar which begins the book, and in which there are indicated the incipits of the chants and lessons for the mass of each feast which has movable parts taken from the common of saints. But in a hand which added the Translation of St. Thomas to the kalendar (*c.* 1220) there are also added, above St. Sixtus et al., and very faintly, the words, 'Transfiguratio Domini', and the incipits of the same mass forms (without prayers) which were used at St. Albans, and later at Lewes, Pontefract, and Barking. In a kalendar of a mid thirteenth-century St. Osyth's psalter the Transfiguration is not included;[2] nor is it in a kalendar of the fourteenth century or a processional of the fifteenth century from the same house.[3]

At Barnwell the feast was celebrated in 1295, as a double;[4]

[1] Bodl. MS. Laud misc. 240. Ker rejects the attribution to St. Osyth's, on the grounds of insufficient evidence, contrary to Frere and van Dijk (and also to F. C. Eeles, *Holyrood Ordinale*, xxix, where he places Laud misc. 240 in the context of other Augustinian service books). An East Anglian Augustinian house in the diocese of London is required; only Colchester, and perhaps Waltham, will do if St. Osyth's be ruled out. The principal evidence against St. Osyth's is that Osyth appears in the kalendar (albeit in red) *after* Marcippus et al. (Oct. 7th); that her Translation is not in the kalendar at all; and that there is no entry in the martyrology concerning her. But her feast is included in the select list of feasts in the chapter homiliary. The Exaltation of the Cross is not included in this homiliary, which would seem to rule out Waltham; the same is true of the omission of St. Botulph for Colchester. The August leaves of the homiliary are missing. The possibility that the various elements—kalendar, martyrology, homiliary—may have been written at different times cannot be excluded; and the absence of the Transfiguration from later St. Osyth texts constitutes probably the largest problem from the liturgical standpoint in making the attribution definite.

[2] Trin. Oxf. MS. 82.

[3] BM MS. Sloane 1935; Bodl. MS. Laud misc. 329.

[4] BM MS. Harl. 3601; kalendar printed in J. W. Clark, *Liber Memorandorum*

since no office for it had been included in the Barnwell antiphoner of the second quarter of the thirteenth century,[1] the date of its introduction there can be fixed to the last half of that century. Earlier in the thirteenth century a Southwark kalendar had included the Transfiguration in the original hand;[2] but even before this, a kalendar of the previous century from Bourne had 'Transfiguratio domini in monte' in green (and therefore important) as the first entry for August 6th.[3] The Bourne entry is puzzling, for it seems to be the exception to the Benedictine and Cluniac origins for the feast in England which we have traced. The Southwark kalendar is not; it is in a volume of annals and chronicles in which Cluniac influence has been strongly suspected.[4] In the kalendar of the 'Derby Psalter',[5] written for Stephen Derby who was prior of Dublin (an Augustinian cathedral priory, like Carlisle) from 1374 to 1379, the Transfiguration follows St. Sixtus in the kalendar on August 6th, but is written, in what appears to be the original hand, in gold letters, to denote an important feast. In general, however, the feast was of no more universal observance among Augustinians than among Benedictines.

For observance in the other orders there is not much evidence either way. Perhaps the most important piece is a Carmelite breviary-missal dating from the late fourteenth century (probably 1375–93), which van Dijk has tentatively ascribed to the Cambridge convent.[6] The Transfiguration has been entered in

Ecclesie de Bernewelle (Cambridge, 1907), 3 ff. Rules for the observances in choir at Barnwell included a provision that the canons should stand at the blessing of fruits which took place 'in transfiguratione', as well as at ceremonies such as the blessings of the palms, the Easter candle, and the paschal lamb: J. W. Clark, *The Observances in use at the Augustinian Priory . . . at Barnwell* (Cambridge, 1897), 90. The blessing of new grapes was a ceremony which had been attached to August 6th (St. Sixtus) from early times, and was simply transferred to the Transfiguration when the latter first replaced the former. The blessing took place before mass, and had nothing whatever to do with the observance of the Transfiguration itself.

[1] As dated by Frere, who edited the MS., CUL Mm. ii. 9: *Antiphonale Sarisburiense* (3 vols., Plainsong and Medieval Music Society, 1901–25).

[2] BM MS. Cott. Faust A. viii.

[3] BM MS. Add. 38819.

[4] M. Tyson, 'The Annals of Southwark and Merton', *Surrey Archaeological Collections* xxxvi (1925), esp. 25–30.

[5] Bodl. MS. Rawl. G. 185.

[6] Univ. Oxf. MS. 9. The argument in Kallenberg, 157, for a date before 1393 is more convincing than van Dijk's date of after 1399, but Kallenberg is clearly wrong in suggesting a Kentish provenance. The book is certainly Carmelite and East

the kalendar by the original hand, coloured red, with the word 'semi-duplex' crossed out. The office contained in the sanctorale is the same as that in the Carmelite ordinal which Sibert de Beka compiled around 1312.[1] It seems to be based on the office of the Trinity, from which many of its parts are drawn. We noticed this connection earlier in John of Würzburg's description of the observance at Jerusalem, which is striking here because the Carmelite liturgy developed from the Jerusalem rite, and seems to have included the feast of the Transfiguration from the beginning. In the few places where the Carmelite office differs from that outlined in the thirteenth century 'Barletta' ordinal of St. Sepulchre,[2] as in the lessons and the antiphons at lauds, the Jerusalem office is even more directly borrowed from that of the Trinity. In both rites the feast had the rank of a semi-double. The mass described in Sibert's ordinal is specified in the Cambridge(?) book; it has more affinities than does the office with the corresponding Cluniac-Sarum service, but is distinguished by its own collect (as in the office).[3] The English book omits the sequence contained in Sibert's ordinal, 'Benedicta sit beata', also borrowed from Trinity Sunday. (We shall see this sequence reappear in the Sarum mass of the Transfiguration.)

One of the few Cistercian books left, a kalendar of the first quarter of the fifteenth century from Calder in Cumberland, has the Transfiguration in black after Sixtus.[4] A good many service books of the Syon Bridgettines survive, but since the nunnery was founded only in 1415,[5] they do not offer much information about observance of the feast before its more general extension. The most concrete fact we have is that by the end of the first quarter of the fifteenth century the

Anglian, or from the diocese of Ely; other possibilities are therefore Lynn, Yarmouth, Norwich, and Ipswich. (It is difficult to establish the provenance of Carmelite books because individual convents do not seem to have had individual dedication-titles.) The presence in the kalendar of several saints especially associated with Ely and the 'Sollempnis marie' on July 17th—commemorating her appearance to Simon Stock in Cambridge—probably points to Cambridge, though very likely all English Carmelite houses would have celebrated the latter feast.

[1] *Ordinaire de l'ordre de Notre-Dame du Mont Carmel par Sibert de Beka*, ed. B. Zimmerman (Paris, 1910), 238.

[2] Ibid. 362: 'Table Synoptique'.

[3] All that is given of this collect is the incipit 'Deus qui te'. There is also an unusual introit, 'Dominus dixit ad me'.

[4] Bodl. MS. Ashmole 6.

[5] At Twickenham (Isleworth); the house was moved to Syon in 1431.

Transfiguration was not being observed, for it does not appear in a processional which can be dated with reasonable certainty to the years 1419–26.[1]

By the beginning of the fifteenth century, then, the Transfiguration was observed in some English Benedictine and Augustinian houses, in all those of the Cluniacs (as far as we know), and probably of the Carmelites as well, and perhaps among those of some of the other orders. Awareness of the feast must have been widespread. What we have now to look at is how, after the papal and local promulgation of the feast, this awareness spread to general observance. These promulgations occurred in two rather widely separated stages. First there was Callistus's bull of 1457, 'Inter divinae dispositiones arcana'.[2] The bull speaks of thanksgiving for the defeat of the Turks (which had actually happened on St. Mary Magdalen's day 1456, but the news was supposed to have reached Rome on August 6th) and orders that the Transfiguration shall be celebrated on August 6th as a double feast, with indulgences similar to those granted for Corpus Christi. It is recognized in the bull that the Transfiguration story was commemorated on Ember Saturday in Lent (and on the Sunday immediately following),[3] but no mention whatever is made of any earlier or existing observance of the feast. This is particularly noteworthy because Alfonso de Borgia, Callistus III, was a Spaniard from Valencia and had been a jurist at the University of Lerida, both among the north-eastern dioceses of Spain, where the Transfiguration had long been observed.[4] (Lerida adjoins the diocese of Vich.) He cannot have been unaware of its observance, but apparently he wished to present the feast as entirely new. This is borne out by the fact that he had a new office and mass composed rather than employing any of the existing forms. (These will be discussed later.)

No legislation on a provincial level seems to have been made in England following this bull, for nearly thirty years. We know about what happened then only in a roundabout way: in 1487 Bishop Stillington of Bath and Wells received a letter from the

[1] St. John's Oxf. MS. 167.

[2] *Bullarium Romanum*, ed. Coquelin, iii (iii) (Rome, 1743), 85–8.

[3] But not in the English missals, which contain a different gospel for the Sunday.

[4] Ferreres, 335.

Bishop of London conveying a mandate from the Archbishop of Canterbury of 19 March 1487, which ordered that the Transfiguration should be kept as a feast of nine lessons on August 7th[1] (sic: undoubtedly a scribal error). This mandate carries the authority of a provincial council, though it is not to be found in Wilkins. The northern convocation acted on the matter two years later: at a 'Provincial Council', as it was called, on 27 February 1489, it was enacted that the Transfiguration should be celebrated on August 6th.[2] This was done at the instigation of Archbishop Rotherham, if his will of 1497 is to be believed: the will is dated 'sexto die mensis Augusti, in festo Translationis (sic) Jhesu, et festo Nominis Ejusdem, quae festa in provincia mea ex decreto meo, et cleri mei assensu, pro perpetua statuuntur (celebranda) . . .'.[3]

The most common, and easiest, way of bringing a service book up to date when a new feast was introduced was merely to note it in the margins of the kalendar. Perhaps this was done by necessity, since the mass and office would not always be easy to come by, particularly in a remote parish church. In a breviary which belonged to Denchworth in Berkshire and was written after 1383 the Transfiguration has been added to the margin of the kalendar, as have the other 'nova festa', but the sanctorale has not been supplemented.[4]

The office or mass may then be added by a third hand—sometimes both: an early fifteenth-century breviary has the mass of the Transfiguration added on a blank leaf in the middle of the book (f. 260), while the office is added in a section at the end with the other new feasts (f. 538).[5] This has also happened in the 'Arlingham' breviary[6] (though it came to Arlingham, Gloucestershire, only in 1502): the Transfiguration has been added to the kalendar in the same hand which added the Holy Name, being a different hand from that which added the Visitation; but after the end of the original book there are

[1] *Register of Robert Stillington*, f. 141 (Somerset Record Society lii, 1937), p. 144, abstracts only, in translation.

[2] *Records of Northern Convocation* (Reg. Rotherham Ebor., f. 246), 203.

[3] *Testamenta Eboracensia* iv. 138. Another use of 'translacio' for 'transfiguratio' can be seen in the kalendar of a Sarum book of hours of about 1500, from north-east England: Bodl. MS. Gough liturg. 3.

[4] Bodl. MS. Lat. liturg. b. 14.

[5] CUL MS. Add. 4500.

[6] Salisbury Cathedral MS. 152.

given, all in the same hand, the offices of the Visitation, Osmund, and the Transfiguration (f. 379), followed by the mass of the Transfiguration, with the sequence, 'Fulget mundo celebris', as in the Barking ordinal and as at the end of the manuscript containing the office of Peter the Venerable. (The only other occurrence of this sequence in England is in a Sarum gradual of the fifteenth century,[1] to which are added chants for the masses of Osmund, the Visitation, the Transfiguration (f. 174), and Kyneburga). In a missal written very close to the time when the Transfiguration was promulgated (it contains both feasts of Osmund in the original hand, and so may well be after 1457), the feast has been added to the kalendar in red—probably, at such a date, indicating that its grading as a double feast was known—and the mass has been inserted after the canon (f. 81).[2] In another missal, with the masses of the feasts of 1415 and 1416 added together in what looks like the original hand, notices of the masses of the three principal 'nova festa' are written in the margins of the appropriate days in the sanctorale, e.g. beside the older masses for August 6th and 7th is added (f. 259) 'Festum transfigurationis domini et de nomine Jesu. Require in fine libri.'[3] These additions, too, look to be in a hand at least close to the original.

By the second half of the fifteenth century, when these manuscript books were being added to, the office and mass of the Transfiguration were pretty well standardized into the forms which can be found in the early printed service books. The final 'Sarum office' and 'Sarum mass' are substantially those deriving from the Cluniac tradition. Frere has pointed out that the mass of the Transfiguration was drawn largely from elements originally belonging to the Christmas masses.[4] This is true, but the selection and conflation were not, for the most part, done in England. The only two possible English contributions were the two elements lacking in the manuscript containing Peter the Venerable's forms. The first, an introit, 'In excelso throno / Jubilate', from the first Sunday after the octave of the Epiphany, is found in the early fourteenth-century St. Albans missal, and an

[1] BM MS. Add. 17001. The addition of Kyneburga points to the neighbourhood of Gloucester.

[2] Bodl. MS. Laud misc. 164.

[3] Bodl. MS. Jones 47. None of the three feasts has been added to the kalendar.

[4] *Sarum Gradual* ii, p. xxvii.

alternative, 'Veni et ostende nobis / Qui regis Israel', from Ember Saturday in Advent, was introduced later, largely in the printed books. The second is at the sequence, where that at the end of Peter's office, 'Fulget mundo celebris' (which we have noted in three English manuscripts, and which is unmistakably about the Transfiguration) is replaced by two more general sequences, 'Laudes salvatori', from the octave of Easter, and 'Benedicta (semper) sit beata / Trinitas Deitas', from Trinity Sunday. Of these two, 'Laudes salvatori' seems to have been used earlier. It appears among the additions to a fourteenth-century missal which belonged to St. Margaret's Lothbury,[1] and is added to a missal of the next century from St. Botolph's Aldgate,[2] while the 'Arlingham' breviary gives it as an alternative to 'Fulget mundo celebris'. There seems to be only one manuscript missal to which a mass with 'Benedicta semper sit' has been added,[3] and in this mass the introit is 'Veni et ostende': a pairing which is contained in the printed books. An addition to a Sarum gradual of the mid fifteenth century[4] contains what seems to be an original sequence, 'Orbis terra renovatur', the most substantial English liturgical composition for this feast, but one which does not appear outside this manuscript. The only other addition of note to the mass is a farsed Kyrie 'Pater (in other versions 'Deus') creator omnium' in a mid fifteenth-century missal from Gawsworth, Cheshire.[5] This is not one of the farsed chants found after Peter's office, but had been in the kyriale of the Sarum missal for a long time.[6] A farsed Kyrie would be an indication that the feast was considered important, which agrees with its addition in red to the kalendar.

The final form of the Sarum office differed from both Peter's office and some of its successors in the third hymn: not 'Deus manens primordium', as in the Pontefract and Barking offices, but 'Caelestis formam gloriae' as at Lewes and Worcester. The lessons of the Sarum office follow the English monastic models in being taken from Jerome and Bede, rather than from the

1 CUL MS. Dd. i. 15, f. 236.

2 Christ Church Oxf. MS. 87. It also appears in CUL MS. Add. 4500, ut. sup.

3 CUL MS. Gg. v. 24, f. 295. This is the sequence which, as we saw, is specified in the Carmelite ordinal of *c.* 1312, though it is not included in the English Carmelite mass for the Transfiguration in Univ. Oxf. MS. 9.

4 Queens' Cbg. MS. 28, f. 261. This sequence is in neither *RH* nor *AHMA*.

5 Bodl. MS. Barlow 1, f. viii.

6 *Sarum Missal*, 929*.

sermons of Peter the Venerable and Leo, though the Sarum lesson vii is cap. i of Leo's sermon. The eighth and ninth lessons are a curious mixture of Bede on Mark as in the Pontefract office, Bede on Luke,[1] Bede on Mark again, and further verses from Jerome on Matthew, which has provided the lessons of the first two nocturns. This is, of course, true only for the longer lessons of the choir breviaries.[2] In a portable breviary, such as one which will be discussed more fully in the next chapter,[3] the lessons start out on the same principle, but are only half as long, or less; in this case, the end of lesson vi in the portable breviary is about a third of the way through lesson iii of the printed choir editions. A new start is then made in the third nocturn, which normally follows the strict pattern of a commentary on the gospel, but the three lessons of the shorter version only equal lesson vii of the longer.

By the time, then, that printed service books were introduced, the forms of the Sarum mass and office were standardized, and the feast was, we can fairly conjecture, in the process of being generally accepted. The Transfiguration is in the kalendars of all the printed Sarum missals, in red except for a few editions (notably the 1488 and 1492; the 1494 edition is the first to have it in red). The alternation of the two introits 'Veni et ostende' and 'In excelso throno', and to a lesser degree of the two sequences 'Benedicta semper sit' and 'Laudes salvatori', makes an interesting pattern. The earliest editions have 'Veni et ostende'; 'In excelso throno' first appears in the 1500 London edition, and succeeding editions have one or the other in about equal numbers until the 1526 edition. From then on 'Veni et ostende' is used in every edition except for the very last, that printed in London in 1557. Most editions mention both sequences. Five of the early ones (1488-98) give 'Benedicta semper sit' alone—in

[1] *Sup. Lk. III*, ix *PL* xcii. 456.

[2] Obviously, the longer versions of the lessons are the 'originals' even though they may be seen less frequently or survive only in later books than their abridgements. A Sarum lectionary of about 1400 (Bodl. MS. Auct. E. 1. 1) has three sets of additions by different hands: David, Chad, John of Beverley, Winifred; Translation of Osmund, Nicholas, Translation of Becket; Visitation, Transfiguration (f. 339v), and Holy Name. The lessons for the Transfiguration are of the same length (though divided somewhat differently) as those in the printed choir breviaries, except for the last three lessons, which only go as far as the printed lessons vii and viii.

[3] Bodl. MS. Lat. liturg. f. 29, f. 181.

each case, and also in the other two editions of which this is true (1501 Rouen, 1519 Paris), in conjunction with the introit 'Veni et ostende', which we noticed also in a manuscript missal. Likewise, every one of the editions which specifies 'In excelso throno' as the introit has 'Laudes salvatori' as the only sequence. The other editions (which all have 'Veni et ostende') refer to the two sequences.

Five of the seven earliest editions of the Sarum breviary survive only in such fragmentary states that it is impossible to tell whether the 'nova festa' were included in them. The earliest edition to survive more completely, 1493 Venice, does not contain any of the three. The 1494 Paris edition, however, has all three feasts in the kalendar in red and with offices in their proper places in the sanctorale. (This breviary has a rubric at the end of the Transfiguration office stating that second vespers is to be said 'ubi ecclesia in honore transfigurationis dedicatur';[1] otherwise it gives place to first vespers of the Name of Jesus.) In the editions from 1495 onwards the Transfiguration is included like any other lesser double feast, without any special notice.

It is clear that by 1495 the feast is fully integrated into the Sarum use (which is, of course, not the same as being everywhere observed). Separately printed editions of the 'officium Transfigurationis' were issued in (probably) 1483, (probably) 1491, and 1496. The latter date indicates the latest it was profitable to print a supplement to breviaries which did not include the feast. Virtually all the other kinds of printed Sarum service books (i.e. besides missals and breviaries) contain some mention of the Transfiguration. This is true of editions of the antiphonal, gradual, legendary, diurnal, psalter from 1506 (the 1490? and 1504 editions do not have it in their kalendars), hours, and processionals. (The processional chant given in the 1519 edition begins 'Videns petrus moysen et helyam in gloria'; this represents a change from the chant added to a manuscript processional of the late fourteenth century,[2] which commences 'In die pater de celis testificatus est filium'.) Of the two earliest editions of the 'Expositio Hymnorum et Sequentiarum', both 1496, that printed at Cologne(?) contains no hymns for 'nova festa', but Pynson's has a supplement with hymns not only for

[1] The question of 'dedications to the Transfiguration' is discussed in Chapter vi.

[2] Corpus Christi Oxf. MS. 18, f. 140.

the Transfiguration, Visitation, and Holy Name, but also for Corpus Christi, St. Anne, St. Mary Magdalen, the Holy Ghost, and St. Vincent. A similar supplement containing sequences for the same feasts appears after the regular sequences. The rubric explaining the supplement makes no mention of new feasts; it simply states, 'sequitur (sic) hymni complures in precedenti libro deficientes'. The same supplement appears in all succeeding editions, whether of exposition, hymns and sequences only, or hymns alone. The only difference from the first edition is that whereas there the table of contents precedes the supplement, in other editions the supplement precedes the table of contents, and is thereby more fully integrated into the book.

There were of course many fewer York and Hereford books printed, and the position with regard to them is consequently simpler. All five editions of the York missal (1509–33) include masses for the 'nova festa' at the end of the book, after the colophon (except in the last edition which has no colophon). There are no new feasts in the first edition of the York breviary, 1493, and the second, 1507, survives only in too highly defective a form to tell. The Transfiguration first appears in the 1526 edition, and remains in those of 1533 and 1555. There is no mention of the feast in either the hymnal or the hours of York use, both printed in 1517, nor in the processionals of 1530 or of 1555.

Though the Transfiguration is not in the kalendar of the only printed Hereford breviary, 1505, the office, identical with the Sarum, is in the sanctorale; but it does not appear in either of the editions of 1502 or 1510 (these dates are conjectural), of the missal. What this means in terms of actual observance is hard to say. Anyone following the Hereford use from printed books between, say, 1510 and the suppression of all uses save the Sarum in 1543, would find himself with an office to recite on August 6th without any corresponding mass, and would presumably have to celebrate the mass of St. Sixtus. Such a lack of correspondence must have happened frequently when manuscript service books were everywhere in use, but would have seemed increasingly glaring as printed books brought about more standardization.

One other English printed service book needs to be

mentioned, the 'Abingdon breviary' of 1528. Although a complete copy does not exist, enough survives to show that the Transfiguration was celebrated at the abbey with 'Caelestis formam gloriae' as the third office hymn, rather than 'Deus manens primordium'.

In both York and Hereford uses the forms for the Transfiguration were identical with those of Sarum. Only in Scotland was there any noteworthy variation. Though the Aberdeen breviary contains the Sarum office, the mass in the Arbuthnott missal is totally different—the most striking divergence of this book from its Sarum model. The mass is, in every respect except the apparently unique Arbuthnott collect, that which was composed at Callistus's request, probably by Jaime Gil, the Spanish Dominican who held the position of Master of the Sacred Palace.[1] (We know that Gil wrote the office; his authorship of the mass is inferential.) The mass and office have sometimes been attributed to Callistus himself, but wrongly.[2] Indeed, there are a number of puzzling features about these service forms and their commissioning by Callistus. We have already seen that he must have known the Transfiguration had long been observed in Spain. Gil came from Játiva, and must also have known the old service forms for the feast. Ferreres has suggested that Callistus wished to magnify his part in the victory of Belgrade,[3] and this suggestion is supported in an oblique way by the anonymous continuator of the *Brut*, writing in about 1460:

> This Calist was a Catalane, & an olde man when he was chosen, & continually seek; wherefore he might not performe his zele & desire that he had conceyved against the Turke, & the cause of lettyng thereof was his age & sekeness. This Calixte instituted & ordeyned the Feste of the Transffiguracion of our Lord to be hallowed on Seynt Sixt day in August because of the gret victory that thei of Hungary had ageynst the Turks . . .'[4]

But whatever Callistus's motives, the fact is that not only in Spain but throughout Europe it was known that the

[1] R. Creytens, 'Les Écrits de Jacques Gil, O.P.', *Archivum Fratrum Praedicatorum* x (1940), 158.

[2] Most recently by Holweck, *CE* xv. 19 following Wadding loc. cit. (see note 1, p. 13).

[3] 'La Transfiguration de Notre Seigneur . . .', *Ephemerides Theologicae Lovanienses* v (1928), 637.

[4] *The Brut or the Chronicles of England* ii (EETS cxxxvi, 1908), 522.

Transfiguration was a feast which was celebrated on August 6th, even though it was not widely observed. For example, in the *Legenda Aurea* (mid thirteenth century) the account of St. Sixtus concludes with the remark 'In hac die festum transfigurationis'.[1] The feast may even have been recognized in an oblique way by a predecessor of Callistus. It was thought by at least the eighteenth century that when the canonization of Dominic was in progress (1234), Gregory IX had moved the proposed feast day from August 6th, when Dominic had died, to the 5th to avoid conflicting with the Transfiguration.[2] Gregory's bull, however, gives no reason for the shift of date,[3] but this rather curious piece of information may indicate a tradition that papal cognizance of the feast had taken place more than two hundred years before Callistus's 'institution'. This may also help explain the statement sometimes made, that Callistus intended his new services to be used only for churches which had not hitherto celebrated the feast.[4] There is one additional puzzle, which will be discussed at greater length in Chapter VI. This is that there is some confusion between the Transfiguration and a 'Festum Salvatoris', the latter being—among other things—a dedication feast probably connected in the first instance with the Lateran basilica. The octave which Callistus provided without making obligatory is, for example, especially recommended to churches dedicated to the Saviour: 'Qui vero devotionis causa huiusmodi festivitatis octavas duxerint celebrandas et maxime in ecclesiis sub ipsius salvatoris invocatione fundatis . . .'.[5]

But neither of these factors—extension of the feast to churches where it had not been observed, and a special importance for churches dedicated to the Saviour—explains why in England services of monastic origin and of comparatively limited employment should have been taken into the Sarum (and York and Hereford) use rather than those forms prescribed by the pope. For this, the influence of the earlier English monastic

[1] pp. 483–4 (cap. cxiv).

[2] Benedict XIV, *De Festis* (*Opera*, vol. ix; Rome, 1767), 146 (bk. I, cap. 15, no. 20). Dominic's feast day was later moved back to the 4th, to make room for 'S. Maria ad Nives'.

[3] A. Walz, ed., 'Processus Canonizationis S. Dominici apud Bononiam', *Monumenta Ordinis Fratrum Praedicatorum Historica* xvi (1935), 193. The editor remarks simply that at the time August 6th was taken up by the feast of St. Sixtus.

[4] Ferreres, op. cit. 637.

[5] *Bull. Rom.*, ed. Coquelin, iii (iii), 88.

observance must be held responsible. Nor is it clear why the Arbuthnott missal of 1491 has the Roman mass (printed at the end of the first edition of the Roman missal in 1474), while the printed Aberdeen breviary of 1510 employs the Sarum office rather than the Roman, i.e. Gil's.

Even with service forms standardized and appearing in virtually all the editions of printed service books, acceptance of a new feast like the Transfiguration was by no means uniform in date or universal in extent. A book of hours from a cell of Malmesbury abbey at Pilton, dated 1521, does not contain the feast in its kalendar.[1] The same is true of a manuscript Sarum missal of the fourth quarter of the fifteenth century—the earliest obits and birthdays date from 1485—belonging to the Carew family.[2] And not only in places which were perhaps rural backwaters was the feast ignored. At a visitation of Eton in 1530 it was found that the Transfiguration and the Name of Jesus were not being kept at the College; the excuse given by a chaplain is a rather surprising one, 'ob defectum librorum'.[3] It is hard to imagine this as a valid excuse at such a late date, but the fact that it was offered may give some clue to why the acceptance of a new feast seems sometimes haphazardly irregular.

Occasionally we have a precisely dated observance, or recognition, of the feast. In 1498 one John Pullan wrote to Richard Plumpton, the chaplain of the Plumpton family, enclosing 'the fest of *Nomen Jesu* with Utas (octave), and also the fest of the Transfiguration, that ye desired me to send you. As for the price of them, ye and I shall agree at our next cominge togither.'[4] In the accounts of the church of St. Mary at Hill in London in 1510–11 four pence is recorded 'for brede, ale and wyne at the fest of the Transfiguracion'[5]—presumably for bell ringers, as a more explicit entry makes clear for All Saints Day—but why special ringing should have taken place on August 6th is not explained.

It seems fair to say that the Transfiguration came to be observed in England in three stages. First there was a sporadic

[1] Bodl. MS. Rawl. liturg. g. 12.

[2] Bodl. MS. Laud misc. 253.

[3] *Visitations in the Diocese of Lincoln 1517–31* ii (Lincoln Record Society xxxv, 1944), 137.

[4] *Plumpton Correspondence* (Camd. o.s. iv, 1839), 130.

[5] *Medieval Records of a London City Church* (EETS cxxviii, 1905), 274.

monastic observance, perhaps originating at St. Albans, but most consistent among the Cluniacs. Service forms employed clearly came from, or through, Peter the Venerable. This early observance was shared by some other religious houses, notably among the Benedictines and Augustinians. The second stage follows on Callistus's institution, or universal extension, of the feast in 1457. The monastic service forms which had been used in England since the thirteenth century begin to appear in English secular books, rather than the forms which Callistus had had composed. Just how widely the feast spread in the thirty years after papal promulgation is uncertain; in the third stage, which begins with proclamation of the feast by synods of the two provinces in 1487 and 1489, there is much wider diffusion, coinciding with and aided by the appearance of printed service books, with the standardization of forms they made possible. But even at the end of the period the feast was not everywhere observed in England; and its spread shows the characteristically untidy features of medieval liturgical development in contrast to Reformation and counter-Reformation liturgical uniformity.

III

THE FEAST OF THE VISITATION

THE history of the feast of the Visitation in the West stretches back officially only to 1389, when it was instituted by Boniface IX, in accordance with the wishes of his predecessor, Urban VI, who had begun the project in the same year. Boniface's bull, 'Superni benignitas conditoris', states the purpose of the feast: to implore the aid of the Virgin Mary towards ending the Schism.[1] Indulgences were granted for the new observance, which was equipped with both vigil (which would conflict with the octave of John Baptist) and octave, and the date of the feast was set at July 2nd. This feast would appear to be a rare example of a new liturgical observance established solely by the fiat of authority. Though it is difficult to credit that what seems in many ways so obvious a celebration—the story of the Virgin's visit to Elizabeth is full of picturesque tenderness and, as the original occasion for the Magnificat, of liturgical appositeness as well—should have come into being so relatively late, and without a long period of unofficial or popular observance (as in the case of the Transfiguration and the Name of Jesus), no hints of any markedly earlier observance prove convincing.

There is a rather distant Eastern analogue. The commemoration of the translation of the Virgin's mantle, which had been miraculously deposited in Palestine, to Constantinople some time in the third quarter of the fifth century, was an Eastern feast of considerable antiquity, chiefly observed on July 2nd.[2]

[1] *Bullarium Romanum Taurinensis* iv (Turin, 1859), 602–4; *AA. SS.* Jul. i. 296. The supplement to the *Legenda Aurea*, 884 ff., states that Urban originally established the feast after the Annunciation, but since dates at that season often conflicted with Lent or Passiontide observances, it was moved to July 2nd; what this probably alludes to is that Boniface's bull, referring to Urban's institution, was to have effect from 27 March 1389.

[2] Janin, 169, 176, 178; cf. his article in *DHGE* xi. 75. There is no evidence for the assertion of the identity of Eastern and Western feasts made by Dom Gregory Dix, *The Shape of the Liturgy* (London, 1945), 376.

The connections between this Eastern feast and the much later Western observance of the Visitation are, then, two: both are Marian feasts; both are celebrated in most places on July 2nd.[1] The first takes us no further, since the two events commemorated have no similarity. But it does seem likely that the date of the Eastern feast influenced the Western date. Without necessarily supposing an explanation as concrete as that the Crusaders brought knowledge of the feast to the West,[2] there must be some reason why it was established on such an unlikely date. There is no suggestion in the Lucan narrative that Mary was present at the birth of John the Baptist (traditionally on June 24th), and given the propensity which existed in the later middle ages for filling out the liturgical cycle of historical (or apocryphal) events in the Virgin's life (e.g. the Presentation, the Compassion, and also the cult of St. Anne), the choice of such an unlikely date is probably due to the knowledge of a Marian observance unparalleled in the West.[3]

Indeed, the early liturgical use of the story in the West was at the temporally logical time, in Advent. By the sixth century, it was the Gospel for Ember Friday in Advent.[4] The commentaries of the earlier fathers on the story had been in the context of Luke's gospel as a whole; but Bede's homily[5] is on the Visitation as an isolated story, perhaps reflecting its use as a pericope. Among Celtic documents, the martyrology of Tallaght has, on December 18th, 'Salutatio Mariae ab Elizabeth matre Iohannis', while that of Oengus includes, on July 1st, 'the marvellous calends of July Mary whom Matthew magnifies',[6] the latter perhaps a reference to the Eastern feast.

The origins of the feast in the West are commonly traced to the Franciscans in the mid thirteenth century, following a

[1] There was considerable variation in the west, right up until the end of the middle ages. At York, as we have noticed, the feast was kept on April 2nd (from 1513); at Prague and Ratisbon on April 28th, Paris June 27th, Reims and Geneva July 8th, Avranches April 1st: Holweck, *Cal. Liturg.* 214, and in *CE* xv. 481.

[2] As is suggested by G. Löw, *EC* xii. 1500.

[3] Cf. H. Thurston, 'The Irish Origins of our Lady's Conception Feast', *The Month* ciii (1904), 459.

[4] T. Klauser, *Das römische Capitulare Evangeliorum* (Liturgiegeschichtliche Quellen und Forschungen xxviii, 1935), s.v. Luke 1: 39–47 in index, p. 189.

[5] *Homilia* II: *PL* xciv. 1 ff.; anachronistically entitled in Migne's edition: 'In festo Visitationis B.M.'.

[6] HBS lxviii. 86; HBS xxix. 160. It is of course Luke and not Matthew who 'magnifies' Mary.

statement of Wadding's[1] that this feast, together with the Conception of the Virgin, St. Anne, and St. Martha, was introduced into the Franciscan liturgy at the chapter general of Pisa in 1263. This statement is now known to have been an error, and the Visitation is not found in Franciscan service books before its general promulgation of 1389.[2]

The first real observance of the Visitation before its papal promulgation seems to have been in Prague, where it was kept on April 28th, probably from 1386, during the archiepiscopate of John of Jenstein.[3] John (who was also chancellor of Bohemia) had a great devotion to the story of the Visitation, and urged universal extension of the feast on Urban and Boniface. In the course of promoting the new devotion John came into controversy with Adalbert 'Ranconis' (Vojtěch Raňkův), active in the Bohemian reform movement, as well as with Raymond da Vineis, master-general of the Dominicans.[4]

Acceptance of the feast after its promulgation in 1389 was limited at the most to the Roman obedience, and within that it was by no means universal. The Franciscans in a chapter general at Assisi in 1390 legislated for its inclusion; one branch of the Carthusians, who had been split by the Schism, accepted the feast, the other did not;[5] the Carmelites recognized it in 1393.[6] The other orders did not for the most part observe the feast until the latter part of the fifteenth century.[7] The Roman curia,

[1] *Annales* ad an. 1263, no. xv (Rome, 1732: iv. 218). Wadding's error is explained by H. Golubovich, 'Statuta Liturgica . . . 1263', *Archivum Franciscanum Historicum* iv (1911), 66.

[2] van Dijk and Walker, 376.

[3] A recent monograph, I. V. Polc, *De Origine Festi Visitationis B.M.V.* (Rome, 1967), is concerned largely with explicating the role of John of Jenstein, and contains no information about the fortunes of the feast in England.

[4] See J. Loserth, 'Beiträge z. Gesch. der husitischen Bewegung I: Der Codex Epistolaris des Erzbischofs von Prag Johann von Jenzenstein', *Archiv für österreichische Geschichte* lv (1877), 265–400, esp. 344–50 and 364; and 'II: Der Magister Adalbertus Ranconis de Ericinio', ibid. lvii (1879), esp. 252–5 and 272–4. For Raňkův see also Emden, *Oxford* iii. 1547.

[5] Hourlier and de Moustier, 157.

[6] Kallenberg, 44, 126.

[7] Among the Dominicans (who, as we shall see, had an office from at least 1399), there was apparently some variation in the dates the Visitation was adopted; at the chapter general at Novara in 1465 it was ordained that 'in conventibus ac provinciis in quibus festum visitacionis b.m. celebrari consuevit, post festum ipsum fiat officium octavarum SS. Petri et Pauli, deinde octave dicti festi perficiantur': 'Acta Capitulorum Generalium O.P.' iii, ed. B. M. Reichert, *Monumenta Ordinis Fratrum Praedicatorum Historica* viii (Louvain, 1900), 292. The Cistercians approved the feast only in 1476 (Backaert, 307).

traditionally conservative, was not observing the feast in 1400, and Boniface's bull was reissued in 1401.[1]

In England no evidence remains of any proper liturgical observance of the feast following the 1389 bull, but there are two interesting notices. A charterhouse at Axholme in Lincolnshire, the first founder of which was Thomas Mowbray in 1396, was dedicated to the Visitation. The idea was put forth ten years earlier, and a mandate granted by Urban VI; this was renewed by Boniface, who in 1398 allowed the special indulgence called the 'Portiuncula' (granted originally to those visiting the church of the village where St. Francis made his headquarters), towards the foundation of the house. The indulgence is limited to those who shall visit and contribute to the Chapel of St. Mary 'in festo Visitationis ipsius beatae Mariae quod secunda die mensis Julii inibi annuatim celebratur'; anyone, therefore, who wanted the benefits of the indulgence would have had to recognize, if not to observe, the feast.[2] Unfortunately, virtually no English Carthusian service books which would show whether the feast was liturgically celebrated have survived. At St. Albans Thomas Walsingham recorded the new feast in his account of the year 1392, under the title 'de Salutatione Beatae Mariae', 'qua salutavit Elizabeth, cognatam suam componens lectiones et historiam competentem, plenam mysteriis, refertam indulgentiis, excitativam devotionis'. He notes the indulgence, as for Corpus Christi, and the date, which he explains 'quia eo tempore Sancta Maria mansit cum Elizabeth et ministravit ei'.[3]

We know a good deal about the composition of the liturgical texts for the Visitation, and it is interesting to see how their proliferation is connected with the spread of the feast. When the

[1] See references in P. Batiffol, *Histoire du bréviaire romain* (3rd edn., Paris, 1911), 256, n. 2.

[2] M. Thompson, *The Carthusian Order in England* (London, 1930), 220 ff. Boniface's mandate is summarized in *CPL* iv. 537; his indulgence is printed in Dugdale vi. 26. Cf. *VCH Lincs.* ii. 158 ff. According to Miss Thompson, Urban's mandate is in the Public Records Office, Exchequer K. R., Eccl. Docs. 2/24: Thomas Mowbray proposes to found the Charterhouse '. . . for the special devotion he has to the Visitation'. Where Mowbray might have acquired this 'special devotion' is a puzzle. The record of his activities (*DNB* xiii. 1127–33) gives no hint of how he might have encountered the new feast, unless possibly through Anne of Bohemia or her Bohemian followers. Mowbray had as a young man been very close to Richard II.

[3] *Historica Anglicana* ii (RS xxviii/1b, 1864), 207.

feast was promulgated rhythmical offices were much in vogue, and at least eleven were composed for it in the century after 1389.[1] Three were completed within a decade after the bull, at the latest. John of Jenstein had written (perhaps before the bull) an office 'Exurgens autem Maria', and also three hymns, three sequences, and two tropes. But, despite his influence in getting the feast declared, the office which was most widely accepted in the Roman books was that of the English Benedictine, Adam Easton.[2] Easton was one of the cardinals imprisoned and tortured by Urban, and, though he escaped with his life (partly through the influence of Richard II), was deprived of his dignities by Urban probably in 1386; these were restored in the first year of Boniface's primacy, and it is therefore overwhelmingly likely that Easton wrote his office for Boniface rather than for Urban. The office is ascribed to him in a manuscript antiphoner of 1397, the year of his death.[3] The third contemporary rhythmical office, 'Collaetentur corda fidelium', was composed by the same master-general of the Dominicans, Raymond de Vineis, alias de Capua, who had tangled with John of Jenstein over the introduction of the new feast. The office was largely used by Raymond's order.[4]

For fifty years the Visitation had been promulgated, though not everywhere observed, in the Italian obedience, but not in the French. Observance of the new feast had not noticeably helped to end the Schism. The Council of Basel took up the matter in the days of its declining influence. In 1441, at the forty-third session, the council passed a decree, 'Inter assiduas militantis ecclesiae turbaciones', ordering observance of the Visitation on July 2nd, in the hope of ending the Schism: 'ut honorate in hac celebritate . . . (Maria) sue intercessione concilians pacem et unitatem fidelibus largiatur'.[5] No mention is

[1] Ten printed in *AHMA* xxiv. 89 ff.; John of Jenstein's (the rhythmical parts) in *AHMA* xlviii. 427.

[2] A number of incorrect statements about Easton's career are common, particularly that he was bishop of either Hereford or London. In fact, the highest English preferment he received was the Deanery of York, which he seems to have held from 1382 to 1389: see R. L. Poole in *DNB* vi. 33–4, and Emden, *Oxford* i. 620–1. Easton's office is printed in *AHMA* xxiv. 89.

[3] Ibid. 92–3: MS. Raigradense FK 1 a 2.

[4] Ibid. 94; cf. P. Mortier, *Hist. des Maîtres Généraux de l'Ordre des Frères Prêcheurs* iii (Paris, 1907), 646.

[5] *Monumenta Conciliorum Generalium seculi decimi quinti* iii (Vienna, 1886), 959–61.

made of Urban or Boniface, or of the fact that there had been any previous observance of the feast at all. Yet the dissatisfaction of those (the Germans, including Bohemians) who wanted an observance which they already cherished to be made universal, was the primary reason the question had been brought up—and in fact brought up again and again, since its solution did not seem easy.[1] After the decree was passed, preparation of an office and mass was entrusted to Thomas de Courcelles, who had played a prominent part in the initial deliberations. It was not until 1443 that Thomas reported back, and on June 28th the council accepted the service forms which he submitted. The office, 'in splendoribus sanctorum', is a sober compilation, not rhythmical and not very original: the hymns are a reworking of Aquinas's hymns for Corpus Christi, with a bare minimum of changes.[2] The lessons are merely the council's decree divided into nine sections, and no octave is provided for. It would be interesting to know (as it does not appear that we do) which forms had been used at the council in 1441, before Thomas de Courcelles had done his work, for a celebration of the feast took place in that year, after the decree had been passed: 'Pro executione autem die isto cardinalis Vicensis vesperas et sequenti missam celebravit sollennem de festo visitacionis'.[3]

At this point acceptance of the Visitation ought, strictly speaking, to have been universal. But this was so far from being the case that Sixtus IV virtually re-established the feast. Sixtus, like many other Franciscans, was active in promoting devotion to the Virgin,[4] and in 1475 instituted the feast of the Visitation anew, this time to invoke Marian aid against the Turks.[5] Yet another rhythmical office, 'Ut vox Marie', was composed at his

This volume contains John of Segovia's contemporary history of the council, through which the story can be traced, supplemented by J. Haller et al. ed., *Concilum Basiliense. Studien und Quellen zur Geschichte des Konzils von Basel* vii (Basel, 1936).

[1] See John of Segovia in *Mon. Conc.* (preceding note), 958.

[2] Ibid. 1308. A good example is this stanza from the hymn for vespers: 'Nobis datus et formatus / in electa virgine / Per infantem honoratus / ventre clausum femine / Novi lucem incolatus / grato pandit ordine.'

[3] Ibid. 959.

[4] In 1476 he formally (i.e. papally) instituted the feast of the Conception with proper mass and office.

[5] Raynaldus, *Annales* ad. an. 1475, nos. 34 ff. Sixtus dedicated his church of Santa Maria della Pace to the Visitation (Löw, loc. cit.).

instigation.[1] A Sistine mass, which appeared at the same time, had, as we shall see, a much wider diffusion than the office.

There were, then, three distinct stages in the promulgation of the feast: Boniface IX in 1389, the Council of Basel in 1441, Sixtus IV in 1475.[2] The degree to which the Visitation was accepted after 1389 has been mentioned; after 1441 the French obedience accepted it, and the feast begins to be found in French service books; the decree of 1475 effected observance where there had been none before, including, for the most part, in England. We have seen that, at the least, the Carthusians at Axholme (with their founder and supporters) were committed to recognition of the new feast, and that the chronicler Walsingham at St. Albans had noted it. By 1430 a new altar at St. Albans, which was mentioned in the last chapter, was dedicated jointly to the Transfiguration and the Visitation.[3] Furthermore, in the same year, the office and mass of the Visitation were introduced there: 'In Vigilia Sancti Albani, ad instantiam Fratris Willelmi Wyntreshulle, introducta est Historia Visitationis Sanctae Mariae, de qua in Octabis Sancti Amphibali Missa fuerat primitus decantata in Capella Beatae Virginis solemnitur.[4] William Wyntreshulle must have been specifically devoted to the Visitation, for he appears to have had another altar dedicated to it, in a wing of the old infirmary in which he lay ill, and consecrated by the same bishop who consecrated the first altar, which was near the chapel of St. Mary.[5]

[1] There had already been a Franciscan rhythmical office, 'Candida plebs fidelium', composed by Peter de Candia, who became Alexander V and died in 1410: P. Lampen, 'Prosae seu Poemata Petria de Candia, O.F.M.', *Archivum Franciscanum Historicum* xxiii (1930), 172. This is printed in *AHMA* xxiv. 98–102.

[2] In Wordsworth and Littlehales, 192–3, it is stated that papal sanction for the feast in England was given in 1431. This statement seems a total enigma, unless it could be a misprint for 1481.

[3] *Amundesham Annales* i (RS xxviii/5a, 1870), 50.

[4] Ibid. 52.

[5] Ibid. 449. From Appendix D: 'De altaribus, monumentis, et locis sepulcrorum, in ecclesia monasterii sancti albani, quaedam annotationes' (BM MS. Harl. 3775, f. 129). 'Est insuper in ala partis corporis Infirmariae antiquae Monasterii, ubi infirmi jacere solebant, altare per Willelmum Wyntreshulle, gistarium ibidem, erectum, et ejus sumptibus et instantia a Domino Willelmo, Dei gratia, Cestrensi Episcopo, in Honorem Sanctae Mariae Virginis, sub titulo Festi Visitationis Elizabethae, consecratum'. It is just possible that these two altars may have been the same, the original one in the old infirmary having been moved to the vestry at the south-east corner of the Lady Chapel, which was added in about 1430 (*VCH Herts*. ii (1908), 487); the chapel could then have been reconstructed and given an additional dedication to the Transfiguration. But it is not necessary to suppose that

Wyntreshulle spent the whole of his adult life from 1369 until at least 1430, at St. Albans;[1] he was evidently a man of learning and some means, which he used for beautifying the abbey. One can only wonder where he came by his knowledge of the feast (and what prompted his devotion to it—could it have been its ostensibly eirenic purposes?), as well as where he got the text of the office and mass he introduced.

Certainly official observance of the Visitation in England really began only with Sixtus's decree in 1475. Five years later Convocation of Canterbury petitioned the Archbishop to order the feast in his province: 'Et quia nos itaque piis ducti consiliis, dignisque studiis excitati, quod beatissimi patres in apostolatu olim summi pontifices festum visitationis beatissimae virginis mariae auctoritate divina indixerunt . . .'[2] The feast is to be kept as a greater double, on July 2nd, with an octave. At the same time the feasts of Osmund, Etheldreda, and Frideswide were ordered.

Both individuals and parish churches busied themselves to observe the new feast. Edward IV's queen, Elizabeth Woodville, petitioned the pope in 1480/1 that, since certain important English feasts fell within the octave of the Visitation—the Translation of Thomas the Martyr on July 7th is the only specifically English feast, but the Translation of Martin on the 4th and the Octave of Peter and Paul on the 6th would also have to be observed, both being feasts of nine lessons—it was impossible to gain the indulgences attached to the keeping of the full octave. Sixtus replied that private recitation of the

the altar was moved from the old infirmary, part of which was left standing when the new one was built between 1260 and 1290 (ibid. 509). The statement there that Wyntreshulle's altar was set up during the abbacy of Thomas de la Mare, 1349–96, is evidently a mistake, in view of Wyntreshulle's introduction of the Visitation in 1430 and of the fact that he is described as 'gistarius', i.e. bedridden, which would better suit his seventy-sixth year—he was born in 1354—than at most, his forty-second. There is one other possibility: that the chronicler who described the altar near the Lady Chapel as dedicated to the Transfiguration and the Visitation may have been conflating two new altars, Wyntreshulle's dedicated to the Visitation, and Thomas Westwode's to the Transfiguration. There is no reason, except novelty, for combining the two dedications in one altar, and besides, we have seen that in 1430 the Transfiguration was by no means a new feast at St. Albans. Into the list which comprises 'Appendix D', a notice of the Transfiguration altar has been added, and there its dedication is given as 'In honore Sancti Salvatoris et Transfigurationis' (p. 445). (This dedication will be noticed again later.)

[1] Emden, *Oxford* iii. 2127.

[2] Wilkins iii. 613.

office on the days when public observance of other feasts was enjoined would secure the full indulgences.[1] In the same year the churchwarden of St. Edmund's, Salisbury, paid 'for viii quayres of velom bought to write the Visitacion of oure Lady and Seynt Osmund stories to the use of the Church vi. s. It. paid to Sir John Odlond for wryting of the same ingrosse v. s.'.[2] Two years later twenty pence were paid 'for the byndyng of a newe boke yn the whiche is conteyned the legende of the visitacion of oure Lady wt the legendes of other dyverse ffestes'.[3] In 1483/4 a further sum was spent 'Pro tribus quaternis de commemoracionibus Sci Edmundi Sci Osmundi et Visitacionis beate Marie Virginis iii s. iiii d.', and two more shillings were spent in 1495–6 'pro facture duorum novum festorum viz. de Visitacione beate marie & de Sancto Osmundo'.[4] Finally, sometime after 1483–4 six shillings were paid at Tintinhull (Soms.) 'pro scriptione Visitationis beate Marie et Beate Anne'.[5] The Lady Margaret Beaufort, Henry VII's mother, provided herself some time before her death in 1509 with the 'history of the Visitation' along with the 'history of the Name of Jesus', both written for her by Dr. Henry Horneby, her secretary, later Master of Peterhouse. Bale says this 'Historiam Visitationis' began 'Aeterni patris filius Mariam'.[6]

The office which begins with these words is distinctive to the Sarum, York, and Aberdeen breviaries. By whom, when, and where it was composed are questions on which little light is shed by internal evidence. It is to be found in manuscript breviaries, chiefly among additions, but is in its proper place in the sanctorale in the printed breviaries, so it could have been composed after Sixtus's bull of 1475.[7] No office was prescribed by

[1] English summary of Sixtus's decree, 'Desiderantes reddere domino' in *CPL* xiii (i), 90–1. The pope goes on to indulgence the devotions of the Rosary ('quidam modus orandi noviter non sine magna devotione inventus') and the Angelus.

[2] *Churchwardens' Accounts of S. Edmund & S. Thomas, Sarum 1443–1702* (Wiltshire Record Society i, 1896), 23 and 367.

[3] Ibid. 368.

[4] Ibid. 35, 45.

[5] *Churchwardens' Accounts* . . . (Somerset Record Society iv, 1890), 194. If this is to be taken literally, the insertion of the feast of St. Anne was made a full hundred years after it was decreed!

[6] *Script.*, pt. ii. 72. We shall consider later how likely Horneby's authorship is.

[7] The most substantial objection to a late date is the Sarum breviary (Bodl. MS. Lat. liturg. f. 29) which bears the date 1443 in the scribe's hand on the last page of the original text. In this breviary 'Aeterni patris' is in sequence in the sanctorale (f. 60^{v}), in the original hand with a footnote added by another hand giving

Canterbury Convocation in 1480, and it is clear that 'Aeterni patris' is not the only office which was known in England. In the large noted breviary which, it has been suggested, was at some time in use at Launton in Oxfordshire,[1] two offices of the Visitation have been added in a section at the end, which also includes offices of the Transfiguration and the Holy Name: 'Aeterni patris', with music, is one, but first comes 'Ut vox Marie', without music. This latter office is the one particularly associated with Sixtus, and it is almost certainly not older than 1475; it is referred to in the Roman breviary printed at Venice in 1534 as 'Officium novum visitationis beate virginis: quod officium instituit sixtus quartus'. The additions to the 'Launton' breviary come in two groups. The first, following on the sanctorale and in a hand that looks identical with the main text, includes synodal services of King Edmund, Deposition of John of Beverley, Translation of St. Nicholas, Dominic with Oswald as a middle lesson, Thomas of Hereford with Leodegarius as a middle lesson, Francis, Translation of John of Beverley, and Winifred (rubricated 'non sarum sed provinciale cantuariensis'); then, after a gap of two lines, which does not exist between any of the synodal services, follows 'Ut vox Marie', in what appears to be still the same hand. It concludes in the middle of the last page of the quire which began in the middle of the office of St. Winifred. The text has been scrutinized carefully after it was written, for the next to the last sentence of lesson iv in the second day of the octave (called here 'prima die') has been omitted by the scribe, but supplied at the foot of the

directions for compline; this would suggest that the office was in existence by 1443. But there are other difficulties in the dating of this book; the Transfiguration and the Translation of Osmund are added in the scribe's hand after the end of the original text, and there is a puzzling prayer for the Deposition of Osmund in the sanctorale. There is no kalendar. The easiest, as well as the likeliest, solution is that the correct date is 1483, a year which corresponds to the dominical letter specified by the scribe ('Explicit in festo sancti Ruphi martiris [August 27th] a.d. 1443 littera dominicalis e') and which makes sense of the other liturgical indications. On this supposition the scribe would simply have duplicated the four instead of writing the correct eight.

[1] Bodl. MS. Laud misc. 299. Ker rejects the attribution, only on grounds of insufficient evidence (private communication). But the book was almost beyond a doubt in use there. There is a notation of the annual fee of 12*d.* which the parishioners of Launton paid to Bicester Priory in return for the right of sepulture which they had gained in 1435 (*VCH Oxon.* vi. 240); and a perpetual obit was founded at Launton in 1522 by Thomas Cottisford, whose son John (Rector of Lincoln College, 1527–32) subsequently owned this book.

page in a contemporary court hand. The sentence supplied agrees with the text of the lesson in the printed Roman breviaries of 1520 (Paris) and 1534 (Venice). After this office there come noted offices for the three principal 'nova festa', all in the same hand (a different one from that of the text and the preceding additions), comprising the last three quires in the book, and decorated rather more elaborately than the rest of the book. The first of the three is 'Aeterni patris', with no indication in the rubrics that another office for the same feast has just been given. This office, too, has been carefully scrutinized: at the end of second vespers (f. 479^{v}) there is a long marginal note, in a different hand from that which copied the office, giving directions for the octave and for compline.

It is curious that the Sistine office did not become standard in England. When in 1480 Caxton printed for the first time an office and mass for the 'festum novum' of the Visitation, he used both Sixtus's mass ("Transite ad me') and the office 'Ut vox Marie'—at least so it seems from the fragments which survive. In all, three supplements containing services for the Visitation alone were printed. Of the second, in 1493(?), probably printed by Mechlin, again only fragments remain, but enough to show that it was the 'Sarum' rather than the Sistine forms which were reproduced.[1] The third, printed in 1495(?) by Pynson, also contains the Sarum office and mass.

Another office which was known in England was the Dominican, 'Collaetentur corda fidelium'. Almost no English Dominican service books of the period have survived, so we do not know whether it was used liturgically, but in a collection of private devotions in a crabbed fifteenth-century hand[2] the office appears, with lessons for the octave and with a mass for the Visitation which differs in some details from the standard mass; then follows Easton's office, 'Accedunt laudes', with nine short lessons. The book in which these are found is largely a compilation of Marian feasts—Purification, Annunciation, Assumption, and Nativity, but not Conception (which is not surprising in a book with any Dominican leanings at all), and also St. Anne and the Eternal Wisdom. It belonged to John

[1] This may well be an indication that the 'Sarum' office was composed between 1480 and 1493.

[2] Trin. Oxf. MS. 13, f. 34.

Leche, who was a fellow of Exeter College in 1458 and of All Souls in 1460, and later held preferments in the West of England, before becoming Vicar of Walden in Essex in 1489.[1] There is no particular reason to think the book was written for him, though his is the only owner's name which appears in it; he is not known to have had any Dominican connections, and all the offices in this book were composed before 1400. But it is noteworthy that he was a canon of Hereford from 1480 until probably 1489, and that it was a peculiarity of the Hereford use that the office of the Visitation was 'Accedunt laudes' instead of 'Aeterni patris'. Among the very few surviving Hereford books, the office appears only in the printed breviary of 1505; but, as we shall notice later, the corresponding mass is included in a manuscript Hereford missal of the early fifteenth century.

A fifth office occurs in one Sarum breviary of the later fifteenth century;[2] it begins 'Pueri laudate', and seems unique to this manuscript. The illuminations are Flemish in style, and the book was bound in Belgium, so it is conceivable that the office may be continental in origin. This is the more likely since one of the two hymns of the office, 'Verbum ex ore prodiens', is also found in a Bruges breviary of 1520.[3] There are no 'nova festa' in the kalendar, and only the Visitation in the sanctorale. This office is a distinctly original one, of some literary pretension.

But all these offices appear only exceptionally. The Hereford rite excluded, the office used throughout the country was 'Aeterni patris'. This was also true in Scotland (where the feast was kept as one which demanded abstention from servile work by at least 1491).[4] The office appears in printed York books after 1513, when the feast was adopted by the northern convocation.[5] Although the length of the lessons at matins often varies from breviary to breviary depending on their sizes, it is striking that the lessons which are inserted in 'Aeterni patris' are totally different in the Sarum and York books. Were the Sarum

[1] Emden, *Oxford* ii. 1120.

[2] BM MS. Roy. 2. A. xii, f. 478v. The rhythmical parts of the office (antiphons, invitatory, responsories) are printed in *AHMA* xxiv. 109–11.

[3] *RH*, no. 21359.

[4] *Arbuthnott Missal*, xciii: 'per statutum Provinciale et Synodale'. The Visitation is in the original hand in the kalendar of the 'Holyrood Ordinale' (ed. Eeles) representing Scottish Augustinian use about 1450, but it is not in the text of the ordinal.

[5] *York Breviary* ii. 735. The first edition of the breviary after 1513 was in 1526.

lessons the 'lectiones et historiam competentem' which Walsingham mentioned in 1392? Probably not, because these lessons are peculiar to 'Aeterni patris', and the chronicler would be likely to have known the office composed by his fellow Benedictine and countryman, Easton. We have seen that the 'historia Visitationis' which Dr. Horneby provided for the Lady Margaret began 'Aeterni patris'. It is just possible that Horneby might have composed this office himself; our earliest authority for this fact, Bale (a generation later), uses the verb 'edidisse', which is ambiguous.[1] But Horneby's authorship is questionable, since he was just starting on his rich career of ecclesiastical preferment in 1481 (when he became a Master of Arts at Cambridge and was given the living of East Deeping in Lincolnshire).[2] It is also somewhat unlikely, as we shall see, that he would have composed as well the office of the Name of Jesus which is covered by the same verb in Bale. However, if the puzzle mentioned earlier—of the breviary which seems to be dated 1443, in the sanctorale of which 'Aeterni patris' appears in the proper place for the Visitation, with extremely short lessons taken from the longer versions found in such choir volumes as the 'Launton' breviary—can be resolved by altering the dating of the manuscript to 1483, it is chronologically possible for Horneby to have composed the office. And why would Bale—unless, of course, he were simply mistaken—have bothered to record, as Horneby's only known writings, works which he had simply copied out, like any common scribe?

The Sarum lessons for the first two nocturns of the feast read rather like a bull, and one would suspect that they might have been taken from Sixtus's bull (which does not appear to be extant, though Raynaldus gives extracts from it),[3] if it were not for the fact that Marian aid against the Turks is nowhere mentioned, whereas the Schism ('virus pestiferum scismatis') is. In the third nocturn the lessons are an extremely skilful condensation of Bede's homily. Lessons on the second day of the octave contain another reference to the Schism, but then continue with a commentary on the Gospel story: not one of the better-known patristic commentaries, but one modelled on their style. It is not until the third nocturn of the Sunday within the octave that

[1] *Script.*, pt. ii. 72.

[2] Emden, *Cambridge* 313–14.

[3] Raynaldus, *Annales* an. 1475, no. 34.

the most widely used of the patristic commentaries on the story, Ambrose's,[1] is employed. (This is in contradistinction to the other offices for the feast, where lessons from Ambrose play a more prominent part). Lesson vi for the Sunday is still concerned with the Schism: 'Iam ergo, mater misericordiae . . . ut quae sola interemisti haereticam pravitatem interimas et scismaticam . . .'. The first six lessons for the octave are still in the form of a commentary on the story and do not differ discernibly from the tone of the lessons at the third nocturn, which are supposed to continue the formal commentary on the Gospel, and which are entitled 'Omelia de diversis tractatibus'. At least one of the 'diversi tractates' is not patristic, for lesson vii concludes 'Hujus sanctissimae Visitationis audivimus hystoriam: imitemur et formam'.

The rubric at the beginning of the office of the Visitation in the (1526) York breviary may give a clue to the origins of its lessons:

> Festum visitationis beate Marie virginis per sacrum convocationem Eborum anno domini 1513 statutum est celebrari ut festum principale iiii nonas Aprilis id est illius mensi die ii. Sicque in kalendario annotandum hujus diei festi plenum hic servitium secundum usum presertim Eborum.

This could imply that there was something peculiar to York about this office; and lesson i for the feast (which has no octave in the York use) begins with what seems a reference to its exceptional, if logical, date at York: 'Celebrantibus nobis nuper fratres Annunciationis dominice festivitatem: convenienter secundum ordinem evangelii subsequitur visitationis solemnitas.' There is no mention, in any of the lessons, of the Schism or popes or indulgences. In lesson vi there is a kind of 'anamnesis' section recalling events in Christ's life, which begins 'Videlicet de parte salubri in nativitate de glorioso nomine Jesu' —perhaps a reference to the feast of the Name of Jesus which had been introduced at York in 1498. The lessons in the third nocturn are from neither Bede nor Ambrose, nor from Jerome's translation of Origen, which is the other commentary on this passage likely to have been used. Throughout, the responsories after each lesson are the same as those after the Sarum lessons; there is no strict integration between lessons and responsories

[1] *PL* xv. 1559.

in 'Aeterni patris' which is violated by the substitution of other lessons.[1]

The fact that the Visitation is frequently the only 'novum festum' added to kalendars leads us to suspect that it was noticed before the Transfiguration and the Holy Name; and the fact that in most of these cases no office or mass has been added points perhaps to a rather more widespread notice than observance of the feast before its official establishment in 1480. Among breviaries, a late fourteenth-century book, which (Ker thinks) may have been used in Salisbury Cathedral and which later belonged to Great Bedwyn in Wiltshire, has the Visitation alone added to the kalendar, with nothing added to the sanctorale;[2] the same is true of another breviary probably from the West of England, written in the early fifteenth century.[3] The colours in which the additions are made to the kalendar contribute supplementary information. The Visitation is sometimes added in red, while the Transfiguration and Holy Name are added in black; this may reflect a difference in the time of addition, since the Transfiguration and the Name of Jesus, especially as they fell on succeeding days, tended to form a pair and were frequently added in the same hand. (The Visitation, as a greater double, should, in a black-and-red kalendar, appear in red, but so should the Name of Jesus.) This is the case with the Denchworth (Berks.) breviary, to which there are additions in the kalendar but not in the sanctorale,[4] as well as with the 'Arlingham' breviary, which was discussed in the previous chapter.[5]

The evidence afforded by (manuscript) missals gives the same impression, that there was considerable awareness of the feast before 1480, but that it is seldom possible to prove, with absolute certainty, observance in any given case. In a number of missals the Visitation is the only one of the principal 'nova festa' to be added to the kalendar.[6] The way in which a mass of the Visitation was added when it was not in the sanctorale gives

[1] The lessons in the Aberdeen breviary (1510) are the same as the Sarum, though re-arranged because of the exigencies of the Scottish kalendar, with one exception: lessons for the third nocturn of the feast are taken from Ambrose (as on the Sunday within the octave, and would thus be repeated if such a day should fall and be otherwise clear) rather than from Bede.

[2] Bodl. MS. e Mus. 2.

[3] BM MS. Add. 32427.

[4] Bodl. MS. Lat. liturg. b. 14.

[5] Salisbury Cathedral MS. 152.

[6] e.g. BM MS. Add. 25588; CUL MS. Ll. ii. 12; Bodl. MSS. Rawl. C. 142, Barlow 5.

some further indication of how it was considered. In several missals the mass is included with those of the Five Wounds, the Holy Name, 'Pro mortalitate evitanda' ('Recordare'), and sometimes with the Transfiguration.[1] In others, the mass of the Visitation appears in a context of new saints' masses: after John of Beverley and before Erkenwald and his Translation, Crispin and Crispinian, and Winifred;[2] or after Mary Magdalen, David, Chad, and Winifred and before the Compassion of the Virgin.[3] The Visitation has been added to both kalendar and sanctorale in so few manuscript missals—only two have been encountered[4]—that it indicates that full integration of the feast was scarcely completed before printed books came into common use (which is borne out by the evidence of the churchwardens' accounts we have seen).

More than one mass for the feast was known in England, though there were fewer masses than offices. The mass which corresponds to the 'Sarum' office is, like that office, probably of English origin. This mass is employed in Sarum, York, and Scottish uses, all with two sequences: the one just referred to, and 'Veni mater gratiae' for the octave day. This latter sequence contains no reference to the Visitation, but is concerned with heresy and schism ('Haereses interime, schismata tu destrue'). The secret and post-communion prayers in this mass also refer to the peace and unity of the church without specifically mentioning the Visitation. A rubric commonly found at the end of the mass enjoins that throughout the octave sequences should be said 'sicut infra octavas Assumptionis ejusdem'.[5] This presumably means the six rather elaborate sequences for each day of the octave of that feast—this would be an indication that the Visitation was of considerable dignity—though in the Sarum missal from Tregaer in Monmouthshire, this rubric is followed by an additional sequence, 'Te regina colimus', which seems to appear only in this book.[6]

[1] e.g. Bodl. MS. Rawl. liturg. c. 3, f. 258; CUL MSS. Dd. i. 15, f. 235v; Gg. v. 24, f. 294; in each of these cases none of the supplementary masses is connected with a date in the sanctorale.

[2] BM MS. Arundel 109, f. 263v, a Sarum missal of 1425 for St. Mary Aldermanbury, London.

[3] Gonville and Caius Cbg. MS. 146 (196), 2nd leaf from end.

[4] Bodl. MSS. Barlow 1, Laud misc. 164.

[5] e.g. BM MS. Egerton 2677, f. 268.

[6] All Souls Oxf. MS. 11; text in *AHMA* xlii. 70.

Only the Hereford use employs another mass, the one which corresponds to its office, Easton's 'Accedunt laudes'. The Hereford mass is the one found in many Roman missals, sometimes with the rubric that it was instituted by Urban VI. There are three variants in the Hereford mass from its Roman form: the psalm-verse at the introit is 'Cantate' rather than 'Eructavit' (the introit is, incidentally, identical in Sarum and Roman masses: 'Gaudeamus . . . / Eructavit'); verse 56 of Luke 1 is added to the standard gospel, verses 39–47; and there is a proper preface, as in the Sarum mass, 'Et te in visitatione'. The sequence, which appears sometimes but not always in Roman and continental missals, begins 'Veni praecelsa domina'. It looks as though the Visitation was accepted into Hereford use in the first half of the fifteenth century, but this conclusion is based on a single piece of evidence, the missal of that date which was used at Whitchurch in Monmouthshire.[1] No other manuscript Hereford missal is extant except one from the fourteenth century which does not contain the feast.[2] A Sarum breviary to the kalendar of which the Visitation has been added (and its octave-day) has on its last leaf, after a series of collects for additional feasts, both the Sarum and Roman collects for the Visitation, marked respectively 'secundum usum Sarum' and 'secundum usum romane ecclesie'.[3]

Among the English Benedictines (and Cluniacs) there was some recognition of the feast, but it was not widespread. One would expect that Easton's office would be used, as in the Hereford rite. There does not seem to be any surviving evidence that this was the case,[4] but the 'Roman' mass corresponding to it was used. It can be found in the fifteenth-century Pontefract missal we have already noticed,[5] and in an addition to a Whitby missal of the middle(?) of the fourteenth century,[6] in each case with slight variations from the Hereford version. The Abingdon missal of 1460–1 presents a curious case; the Visita-

[1] Univ. Oxf. MS. 78A, f. 163^{v}.

[2] BM MS. Add. 39675. But some additions of the second quarter of the fifteenth century have been noted, and the Visitation is not among them.

[3] Peterhouse Cbg. MS. 270.

[4] In the Battle Abbey breviary of the late fifteenth or early sixteenth century (Trin. Cbg. MS. 1359, f. 154) 'Aeterni patris' is used, adapted as an office of twelve lessons.

[5] King's Cbg. MS. 31, f. 132.

[6] Bodl. MS. Rawl. liturg. b. 1, f. 2^{v}.

tion is in the kalendar,[1] coloured blue and marked 'in cappis'; but in the summer part of the sanctorale (which is in the second volume)[2] there is no mass for the feast—nor has it been added anywhere else. It would be stretching a point considerably to insist that this discrepancy indicates precisely the year in which the feast was introduced at Abingdon, but the possibility exists. At Peterborough the Visitation probably did not come into use until very late in the fifteenth century; it has been carefully inserted into a diurnal of the earlier part of the century,[3] in the same way in which the Holy Name has been added (we shall see in the next chapter that this enables us to date these additions). The office is thus made to appear to be in its proper sequence in the sanctorale. Though the first antiphon of the office is that of 'Accedunt laudes' (Easton's), the rest of the office is that written for Sixtus, 'Ut vox marie', in 1475 or thereabouts. If we remember that the office and mass of the feast were introduced in St. Albans in 1430, it will be seen that there was no uniformity in the date of acceptance of the Visitation among the Black Monks.

There are several interesting points about the acceptance of the Visitation among the (Syon) Bridgettines. In the first place, we know the feast was being observed between 1419 and 1426, for the processional which can be dated to those years includes a chant for it in the original hand and in the proper sequence:[4] 'Salve festa dies . . . quo flos de nazareth visitat Elizabeth' (a variant from the usual 'Salve festa dies' continuation, 'Christi mater visitat Elisabeth'). Secondly, the Visitation seems to have been of special importance. A Sarum breviary of about 1400 has been adapted for Bridgettine use by the addition of a supplement at the end, containing lauds for the Commemoration, Translation, and Nativity of Bridget, and for the Visitation;[5] while for the other additional feasts, mostly introduced around 1415—the Eleven Thousand Virgins, David, Chad, Erkenwald, John of Beverley, Crispin and Crispinian, and Winifred—the collects alone suffice. The third point to notice is that the office represented by lauds in this book is somewhat different from

[1] Trin. Oxf. MS. 75. [2] Bodl. MS. Digby 227.

[3] Bodl. MS. Gough liturg. 17, f. 213^{v}.

[4] St. John's Oxf. MS. 167, f. 55. The house at Syon was not occupied until 1431, so this book must have belonged to its predecessor at Twickenham.

[5] BM MS. Roy. 2. A. xiv, f. 279^{v}.

any we have seen before. It is 'Devota visitatio', an office extremely close to, and perhaps merely a version of, 'Aeterni patris', but used on the continent.[1] 'Devota visitatio' is also found in another Syon book, of the early sixteenth century,[2] containing Bridgettine offices for the Nativity of Bridget, and for the Visitation; here there is an unusual hymn at vespers, 'Sacre virginis marie', which seems otherwise to be unknown. In continental books where this office appears the common Marian hymns ('Ave stella maris', 'Quem terra', 'O gloriosa femina') are used.[3] It is possible that this office, like 'Aeterni patris', may have been a relatively late composition: for another Syon office book, of the second quarter of the fifteenth century, prescribes for the Visitation a simple adaptation of an existing Marian office: 'In festo visitacionis B.M.V. totum fiat servicium sicut in festo annunciationis eiusdem', with a few small changes.[4]

At this point we can advance the question about Horneby's authorship a step. Since 'Devota visitatio' is in use in Italy by 1476, if it is an adaptation of 'Aeterni patris' Horneby's authorship of the latter would be a virtual impossibility. If both derive from a common original, now not known—this is the likeliest case, since 'Devota visitatio' is an office of twelve lessons and psalms and 'Aeterni patris' of only nine—Horneby's 'authorship' would be reduced to mere adaptation, but could have taken place any time after 1476. (The third alternative, that 'Aeterni patris' derives directly from 'Devota visitatio', is possible but unlikely, as comparison of the two texts shows.)

The fullest information we possess about acceptance of the Visitation by any religious order in England is of the Premonstratensians. The pages of the *Collectanea Anglo-Premonstratensia* reveal a story both of general adoption of the feast and of its integration into individual houses. The provincial chapter of 1476,

[1] *AHMA* xxiv. 102, where seven instances are cited, all of them offshoots of the Benedictine order (Olivetan, Celestine, Vallombrosan). Bodl. MS. Canon liturg. 168, an Italian Vallombrosan nuns' breviary of 1476, contains the office, with twelve lessons (f. 375).

[2] CUL MS. Ff. vi. 18, f. 150.

[3] But in a fragment of a German breviary of the second half of the fifteenth century, contained in the flyleaves of Bodl. MS. Rawl. G. 48, the hymn at lauds (with which the fragment begins) is 'O salutaris micans', a variant of the Sarum 'O salutaris fulgens'.

[4] Bodl. MS. Rawl. C. 781, f. 75^{v}.

held at Lincoln, ordered the feast to be kept as a triple (a distinctive grading among the Premonstratensians), with a solemn octave.[1] The injunction had to be repeated several times, when visitations showed that the new feast, with others commanded in the same chapter, was not being kept. Halesowen in 1488 was given a generally excellent report, but

districte injungendo precipimus tam abbati quam suis subditis, ut festum cognate beatissime matris Jhesu, Elizabeth, tamquam solempne festum triplicis dignitatis, in crastino octavarum Sancti Johannis Baptiste, cum solempnibus octavis perpetuis temporibus annuatim inviolabiliter celebretur . . .[2]

A similar order had been given at Cockersand in 1481,[3] and it was enjoined at Alnwick in 1491,

. . . ut festa Reliquiarum, sancte Marthe, Visitacionis beate Marie, cum ceteris festis in provinciali Capitulo celebrari ordinata, infra annum propria servicia inde edita et consueta, habere procurent.[4]

What these 'propria servicia inde edita et consueta' were we do not know, and nowhere is it indicated what service forms were to be used.

All the evidence so far has gone to show that the Visitation was accepted quickly and widely in the later 1470s and the 1480s; there do not seem to be such notable exceptions as the failure to observe the Transfiguration and the Holy Name at Eton in 1530 which we saw in the last chapter. The uniformity of the printed service books in consistently including the Visitation corroborates this impression. We saw that three supplements were published containing services for the Visitation only: in 1480, the Sistine forms, and in 1493(?) and 1495(?), the 'Sarum' forms. The first printed Sarum breviary to include the feast is the 1494 Venice edition, as in the case of the other 'nova festa' (but it must be remembered that of the earlier editions only one, the 1483, survives in complete enough form to allow us to say that the feasts were not in it). The Visitation is in all editions of the missals, in red in the kalendar (except, unaccountably, in the 1529 Paris edition), with the two sequences and also with a farsed Gloria, 'Spiritus et alme orphanorum',

[1] *Coll. Anglo-Prem.* i. 141. [2] Ibid. ii. 251. [3] Ibid. ii. 113.
[4] Ibid. ii. 24.

specified for the octave. In the other types of service books the position is much the same as with the Transfiguration. Only the two earliest editions of the psalter, 1490(?) and 1504, and the 1496 Cologne 'Expositio Hymnorum' fail to include it; hymns for the feast are in the other editions of the latter book treated the same way as those of the Transfiguration, i.e. in a supplement. The only textual peculiarity which needs to be noticed is that in the 1530 processional the collect at the procession is 'Vestram continuam' in place of the usual 'Infirmitatem'. The feast is in red in the kalendars of almost all the printed books of hours, and is missing only from the very sparse and Protestant kalendar of the 1539 edition (in English).

Treatment like that of the Transfiguration is also found in the York missals, in all the editions from the first in 1509, and never in the kalendar. The sequence is 'Celebremus in hac die', as in the Sarum books; and a tract is provided because the feast, falling on April 2nd, may well come within Lent. The appearance of the mass in the 1509 edition, after the colophon though it is, is odd, for the feast was not approved by York Convocation until 1513—at least according to the rubric which, we have seen, begins the office in the 1526 York breviary, mentioning the establishment of the Visitation as a provincial feast.[1] The office ('Aeterni patris' with the distinctive York lessons) follows the common of saints in a section which also contains commemorations of the Virgin, William of York, Peter and Paul, and All Saints.[2] The Visitation is in black in the kalendar of this breviary (despite its rank as a 'festum principale'), and in red in the 1533 edition. The latter does not have an office for the feast; a rubric comes at the proper place in the winter sanctorale stating that 'Inter festum annunciationis beate marie et ambrose celebretur festum visitationis beate marie: quod festum invenietur in fine libri', but there is no office at the end. The feast is not included in the York processionals of 1530 or 1555, nor in the hymnal of 1517 nor the hours of the same year. In the *Horae Eboracenses* of 1536 the kalendar entry for April 2nd is Mary of Egypt, and for July 2nd Swithin and Processus and Martinian, as usual in York kalendars. But the mnemonic

[1] No more official record of this establishment seems to have survived.

[2] In the BM copy of the 1526 edition, but the office is lacking in the Bodleian copy. See *York Breviary* i. xvi.

'verse' for July, at the foot of the page, begins 'When Mary visited . . .': an obvious confusion with the Sarum date.

It has already been said that the unique printed Hereford breviary of 1505 contains Easton's office, which is also used in Roman books; the corresponding mass is in both editions of the missal, 1502 and 1510. It is noteworthy that in the office five of the eight responsories after the matins lessons differ from those in the common continental text printed by Dreves and Blume;[1] and that the breviary is dedicated by the printer (I. Haghe of Rouen) to the Lady Margaret, for whom Dr. Horneby is said to have written 'Aeterni patris' and an 'hystoria Visitationis'. The lessons in the Hereford breviary are very brief.

Generally, as has been noted, Scotland followed English patterns in liturgical matters. But in the 'Breviarium Bothanum' of the mid fifteenth century, which, its modern editor points out, follows the Sarum use even more closely than does the Aberdeen breviary, the office for the Visitation reflects French influence, not surprisingly in medieval Scotland. That is, the office for the Visitation (which is original in the sanctorale, as in the kalendar) is that promulgated by the Council of Basel in 1443, 'In splendoribus sanctorum', and which was thenceforth accepted by the French obedience. At the end of the sanctorale, perhaps in another hand (f. 341^{b}; the editor detects fainter ink from f. 288), John of Jenstein's office is given for the vigil of the feast, with three lessons for the Sunday within the octave. There is no explanation of why an additional office should be provided. Whatever may have been the reasons, within roughly half a century (Arbuthnott missal 1491, Aberdeen breviary 1510) the Sarum forms, as we have seen, were accepted.

[1] *AHMA* xxiv. 89; the text in Trin. Oxf. MS. 13 agrees on the whole with this rather than with the Hereford version.

IV

THE FEAST OF THE NAME OF JESUS

THE liturgical commemoration of the Name of Jesus began, not like the Transfiguration and Visitation, as a feast with a place in the proper of time, but as a devotional cult which became liturgical only gradually and by stages. It is possible to trace at least three different emphases which all came to have liturgical expression: in Italy, the emotional, hortatory, and eirenic use of the Name in the preaching of Bernardino of Siena and John of Capistrano; in Germany and the Low Countries, a devotion by comparison austere and nearly neo-Platonic, to the Holy Name as the Eternal Wisdom of God, propagated chiefly by Heinrich Suso; in England, a more comprehensive and balanced (and, one might say, orthodox) Christological approach to Jesus' name in its historical aspect in the Bible. Underlying all three emphases is, of course, the more pathetic and tender devotion towards Christ and his mother which has been commonly traced to the twelfth century, and of which the famous 'Rosy Sequence', 'Jesu dulcis memoria', perhaps by an English Cistercian,[1] is one of the finest products. (Hymns from this composition are found in offices representing all three emphases.)

The cult in England, which most concerns us, had a liturgical aspect from probably the middle of the fourteenth century. A votive mass of the Holy Name is its first expression. This is often found in manuscripts next to the mass of the Five Wounds, another cult resulting from the more personal devotion just mentioned. As in the case of several late votive masses, the indulgences attached to the Jesus mass were an important part of its popularity, and shed some light on its early history.

Robert Hallum, Bishop of Salisbury, granted an indulgence

[1] According to F. J. E. Raby, *A History of Christian Latin Poetry from the Beginnings to the Close of the Middle Ages* (2nd edn., Oxford, 1953), 329. For an extended treatment of the problem, see A. Wilmart, *Le 'Jubilus' dit de Saint Bernard* (Rome, 1944), ch. vi.

in 1411 to all who celebrated or caused to be celebrated the mass of the Name of Jesus: or so it was commonly believed in the fifteenth century. It may well be that Hallum did issue such an indulgence, but it does not appear in his register, which has been recently edited,[1] and the fact that there are a large number of clearly spurious indulgences attached to this mass calls into question the existence of the one ascribed to Hallum. It was common in the middle ages to augment the verisimilitude surrounding a grant of indulgences with the names of popes, more or less indiscriminately bestowed, without regard for historical fact. In the case of the Jesus mass we see a mixture of historical and apocryphal indulgences. (The quite historical indulgences connected with the Name of Jesus from the thirteenth century are concerned not with the mass but with pious ejaculations mentioning the Holy Name, inclinations of the head at such mentions, and the establishment of confraternities of the Holy Name as a weapon against blasphemy.[2] They do not appear to have been current in England.)

Indulgences in English missals for the votive mass of the Name of Jesus take several different forms; the terms vary widely, and so does the authority to which the indulgence is ascribed. An early fifteenth-century missal from the diocese of Norwich contains an indulgence with the most sweeping benefits:[3] whoever celebrates the mass, or causes it to be celebrated, for thirty days (this provision links the indulgences with the fabulous stories of trentals, particularly 'St. Gregory's') will not die 'sine vera contricione et digna satisfactione et sacrosancta communione et sancti olei unctione et infra triginta dies post obitum suum ad gaudia sempiterna perveniet'. In addition, for each such mass three thousand years' indulgence is granted 'a domino papa bonefacio'—which Boniface is not stated; his name, with a variety of numbers, was a popular one for apocryphal indulgences.[4] A slightly later missal, from Gawsworth, Cheshire,

[1] J. M. Wilkinson, 'The Register of Robert Hallum, Bishop of Salisbury 1407–1417' (Oxford B.Litt. thesis, 1959).

[2] See A. Cabassut, 'La Dévotion au Nom de Jesus dans l'Église d'Occident', *La Vie Spirituelle* lxxxvi (1952), 46–69, esp. 56–7 and 68.

[3] Bodl. MS. Hatton 1, f. 219^{v}. Not all Norwich missals contain the indulgence: BM MS. Add. 25588, f. 250, of the early fifteenth century, has added to it the masses of the Holy Name and the Five Wounds, without rubrics.

[4] According to H. E. Allen, *Writings ascribed to Richard Rolle* (New York, 1927), 351.

provides a more impressive pedigree, if less exhaustive benefits, for its indulgence.[1] Here it is St. Peter himself who first grants six thousand years, which is confirmed by the thirtieth of his successors ('a XXXth [sic] sedis apostolice pontificibus et sancti petri successoribus': this would have been Marcellus I, 307–9; why he was chosen is a total mystery) and again by John XXII (1316–34), with slightly different terms: 'tria millia annorum et ccc dies indulgentiae penitencialium et totidem venialium'. Finally, the composition of the mass is attributed to Boniface VI (who was pope for about two weeks in 696): 'Composuit missam subsequentem dans et concedens per potestatem sibi a domino commissam omnibus et singulis qui dictam missam subscriptam affectuose celebraverint aut celebrari fecerint per xxx dies . . . tria millia annorum.'[2]

Hallum's name is brought into this largely apocryphal papal context in the indulgence which follows the mass of the Holy Name in a collection of fifteenth-century theological tracts:[3] it is granted by another Pope Boniface, this time the Fourth (608–15), and four bishops: Hallum; John of Llandaff; John of Elphin; and Cornelius, Archbishop of Tuam. There were bishops of those names attached to those sees in 1411, though Cornelius, a Franciscan, was provided to the archdiocese of Tuam only on 18 September of that year, and his appointment did not take effect;[4] this is doubly curious, because Cornelius would therefore presumably not have been in a position to issue indulgences, and because at least two manuscripts date Hallum's indulgence precisely at 19 July from Sherborne.[5] There seems no logical reason why these bishops should be grouped together by the propagator of a fictional indulgence (if his aim were merely to show that the indulgence ran in England, Wales,

[1] Bodl. MS. Barlow 1, f. 386.

[2] Sometimes only the indulgence is ascribed to Boniface, e.g. BM MS. Egerton 2677, f. 197, a fifteenth-century Sarum missal, and CUL MS. Hh. vi. 15, f. 9, a fifteenth-century collection of masses.

[3] CUL MS. Hh. i. 11, f. 12.

[4] F. M. Powicke and E. B. Fryde, *Handbook of British Chronology* (2nd edn.; Royal Historical Society, 1959), 343; C. Eubel, *Hierarchia Catholica Medii Aevi* i (Münster, 1898), 529.

[5] St. John's Cbg. MS. 201, f. 13, a late fifteenth-century Sarum book of hours; BM MS. Stowe 13, f. 115, a manual, which also includes Boniface's name. Hallum was at Sherborne between 10 July and 23 August 1411: *Reg. Hallum*, ed. cit., 153 contains business which he transacted on 18 and 20 July. In 1411 July 19th was a Sunday, the sixth after Trinity.

and Ireland, why did he include two Irish prelates?), and it is possible that four bishops might issue an indulgence jointly[1]—which could explain why the indulgence is not in Hallum's register. The Archbishop of Tuam from 1407 to 1430 was another John, surnamed Babingle (a Dominican), Cornelius being appointed in 1411 because of Babingle's impending translation, which then apparently never took place.[2] If this indulgence was issued in July 1411, perhaps a scribe, who would be faced with a plethora of Johns which might have looked to him like dittography, could have inserted the name of Cornelius in copying the indulgence a few months later, in order to bring it, as he thought, up to date.

The ascription of the indulgence to Hallum rings true in the limitation of its benefits (bishops could normally grant only forty days) as opposed to the lavishness of some of the more blatantly apocryphal grants. We see this contrast clearly in the indulgence which is in a fifteenth-century collection of masses, where 'Boniface IV' grants three thousand years for each mass, while Hallum allows forty days.[3] This more modest relief is also specified in a mid fifteenth-century Sarum missal, probably from South Yorkshire, which mentions the year 1411.[4] On balance it seems that Hallum probably did issue such an indulgence in that year, and it is conceivable that, considering his sober and reforming bent, he may have done so in order to regularize excessive and fictitious indulgences which were gaining currency. When this mass came to be included in printed Roman missals from about the turn of the sixteenth century, its indulgence was ascribed to Boniface VI.[5]

The mass (which we shall call, as usual, the Sarum mass) so heavily indulgenced is probably not older than the later

[1] No English indulgences are mentioned in the extensive lists compiled by P. Delehaye, 'Les lettres d'indulgence collectives', *Anal. Boll.* xliv (1926), 342–76; xlv (1927), 97–123, 323–44; xlvi (1928), 149–57 and 287–343.

[2] W. Maziere Brady, *The Episcopal Succession in England, Scotland, and Ireland 1400–1875* ii (Rome, 1876), 129; E. B. Fitzmaurice and A. G. Little, *Materials for the history of the Franciscan Province of Ireland 1230–1450* (British Society of Franciscan Studies ix, 1920), 176.

[3] BM MS. Harl. 5444, f. 1.

[4] Bodl. MS. Rawl. C. 142, f. 267.

[5] This indulgence was not confined to the Sarum use; the manuscript Hereford missal of the early fifteenth century, Univ. Oxf. MS. 78A, f. 226^{v}, has a rubric ascribing the indulgence to Pope Boniface. The terms are the same as those of MS. Hatton 1, ut. sup.

fourteenth century, of unknown authorship, and most likely of English origin.[1] Its existence by 1388 seems almost certain: it is appended in what looks like the original hand to a missal prior to that date, written for the family of Beauchamp de Bergavenny;[2] the mass comes after the votives of the dead and before the 'Passion of John XXII'. It is among the votives that the mass is most commonly found in its first stage. Its most typical place is after the series of older votives ('de Angelis', 'Salus Populi', and the like), as an alternative to the earlier Friday votive mass of the Holy Cross; the Jesus mass is then frequently followed by the Five Wounds ('Humiliavit') and 'Pro Mortalitate Evitanda' ('Recordare'). This is the arrangement in a Sarum missal written probably for the monks of Durham:[3] the last two masses are in the same hand as the Name of Jesus.

There is a stage of additions which shows the mass of the Holy Name in transition from a votive to a mass of a feast. The Norwich missal we have already noticed[4] contains no 'nova festa' in its kalendar; after the original text there are added the Visitation, Transfiguration, Name of Jesus, Five Wounds, and 'Recordare'. Though, as we have seen, the indulgence for the Jesus mass in this book speaks of a celebration for thirty days, the Name of Jesus is so placed that it is in a position to be associated as much with the first two of the additions as with the last two. Another indication of this process can be seen in the Cuckney (Notts.) York missal,[5] in which the Name of Jesus follows the Transfiguration; there is no explanatory rubric or indulgence, and at the end of the mass a short rubric deals with how the mass is to be said 'per totas octavas'—a sign that even though there is no mention in the kalendar, celebration of the mass is being regarded as occurring on a fixed day. The rubric for the octave is extremely simple: the mass is to be said without the Creed, and only the last half of the sequence, from the

[1] Miss Allen, op. cit. 350, thought it was 'of general European distribution' (this does not seem to be the case), and was perhaps earlier than Rolle's time. Frere (*Sarum Gradual* ii, p. xxxi) points out that the plainsong music for the Jesus mass was, except for the alleluia, entirely new, which was very rare in the later middle ages.

[2] Trin. Oxf. MS. 8, f. 286.

[3] Bodl. MS. Laud misc. 302, f. 232v.

[4] Bodl. MS. Hatton 1. Another Sarum missal, of the early fifteenth century, has the same arrangement (CUL MS. Gg. v. 24, f. 296); there is no indulgence attached to the Jesus mass.

[5] Univ. Oxf. MS. 78B, f. 154v.

'divisio' at 'Jesus pulcher in decore', is to be used. The addition of the rubricated word 'divisio' in the midst of the sequence is, then, an indication that the celebration of the Holy Name has come to have the character of a liturgical feast. Where such an indication is lacking, as in a fifteenth-century missal,[1] probably from the diocese of Lincoln, where the Jesus mass has been added in the same hand which added the masses of the Wounds and such late-commemorated saints as Sebastian, Anthony, and Gabriel the Archangel, it may be assumed that the Jesus mass was added for the user of the book purely as a votive.

As in the case of the other 'nova festa', the groupings of additions provide information as to how the new mass was considered in each book. The mass of the Holy Name is added to a fourteenth-century missal from the diocese of Worcester[2] along with the masses of saints whose feasts were decreed by Canterbury Convocation in 1415–16, David, Chad, and Winifred. In another missal from the same diocese, to which a great many additions have been made, the mass of the Five Wounds was added in one hand, and the Name of Jesus, the Visitation, and 'Recordare' in another.[3] (Sometimes, of course, a new mass will be inserted wherever there is a blank leaf, as in the missal written for the Carew family towards the end of the fifteenth century,[4] where the Holy Name is inserted after the 'ordo' and the 'cautelae missae'.) Nearly the final stage in becoming a fully liturgical feast is illustrated by a missal[5] to which the three principal 'nova festa' have been added at the end with rubrics in the margin of the sanctorale directing attention to the additions, e.g.: 'Festum transfigurationis domini et de nomine Jesu. Require in fine libri.'[6]

There is virtually no variation in the text of the Jesus mass as

[1] Gonville and Caius Cbg. MS. 146 (196), f. 725.

[2] Bodl. MS. Barlow 5, f. 271.

[3] Bodl. MS. Rawl. liturg. c. 3, f. 256v.

[4] Bodl. MS. Laud misc. 253, f. 121v. There are no 'nova festa' in the kalendar nor, except for the Holy Name, are any masses for them included.

[5] Bodl. MS. Jones 47.

[6] It may be useful to note some negative evidence from two dated service books which survive. A Norwich missal of 1397 (CUL MS. Ff. ii. 31) does not contain the Jesus mass, though that of the Five Wounds is included (in a different hand from the original). In a London missal of circa 1425 (BM MS. Arundel 109) it has not been added, though John of Beverley, the Visitation, Erkenwald, and his Translation, Crispin and Crispinian, and Winifred have. Certainly inclusion of the Jesus mass, even as a votive, was by no means uniform.

found in the missals. The sequence, which is generally included, is 'Dulcis Jesus nazarenus', which the manuscript evidence shows to be English in origin like the rest of the mass.[1] It is paired with the metrical tract 'Dulce nomen Jesu Christi'. The chants are from obvious scriptural texts; the epistle is Acts 4: 8–12, and the gospel Matt. 1: 20–3. (Note the short gospel, which is often found in votive masses.) The prayers are longer and more verbose than most Roman prayers, and are proper to the mass. In some missals there is a proper preface,

Qui gloriaris in consilio sanctorum tuorum tibi enim serviunt creature tue que te solum auctorem et deum cognoscunt et omnis creatura tua te collaudat et benedicunt te omnes sancti tui qui illud magnum unigeniti filii tui nomen coram regibus et potestatibus huius seculi libera voce confitentur. Cui assistunt angeli et archangeli . . .[2]

It is noteworthy that Suso's mass did not establish itself as standard in England. This Dominican mystic had been the great propagator of the cult of the Name of Jesus in Germany and the Low Countries, under the special aspect of devotion to the Eternal Wisdom. He composed both an office and a mass; his office was translated into the vernacular by Gerard Groote in the 1380s, and was known in England in the fifteenth century. In the primer which Wynkyn de Worde printed in 1503 the vespers and compline of Suso's office were ascribed to Richard Rolle, the fourteenth-century Yorkshire mystic who was ardently devoted to the Holy Name, but whose interests were not at all along the lines of liturgical composition.[3] Since the Sarum mass has no similarities with Suso's, it may very probably have been composed before Suso's mass was known in England; otherwise

[1] *AHMA* liv. 174. The ascription often made (e.g. *RH* no. 4909; *CE* vii. 420) to Bernardino da Bustis is impossible on grounds of date alone: he was not born until 1450.

[2] Bodl. MS. Barlow 1, f. 389 (the Cheshire missal with the indulgence ascribed initially to St. Peter, discussed earlier), and Bodl. MS. Laud misc. 164, f. 183, where the preface has been ruled for music, though no notes are filled in. In the margin of the latter, next to the preface, are scratched the words 'Quia per incarnati', the Christmas preface which is the one generally (as in the printed missals) used for this mass. The proper preface also appears in a late fifteenth-century missal (All Souls Oxf. MS. 11), in an Irish missal of the early part of the same century (Lambeth MS. 213), and in the Scottish 'Arbuthnott Missal' (ed. Forbes, p. xcix). It is virtually identical with the preface of the Palm Sunday 'fore-mass' in the (old) Roman rite.

[3] Allen, op. cit. 350. A fifteenth-century theological collection, CUL MS. Kk. vi. 20, attributes the entire office, as well as Suso's mass to Rolle: ibid. 349–51.

it is likely that his mass might have been adopted in the heritage of spirituality which was passing from the Low Countries to England in the fifteenth century.

Nor did Suso's office (dated 1328), which is found in many English as well as continental books of hours, have any influence on the English office (though it is not, as he composed it, suitable for breviary use, being a 'little' or votive office). Like the votive mass of the Holy Name, it was apparently regarded as having no necessary connection with a liturgical feast. This is the case in a fifteenth-century Sarum hours to which Suso's office—'in honore nominis Jesu decantande'—has been added,[1] but there has been no corresponding addition to the kalendar, where the obits of the Hale family (for whom the book was perhaps written) were added steadily after 1489. Several additional feasts—the Visitation, Swithin, Francis, and Hildebert—have been inserted, but not the Holy Name. Suso's office is also found at the end of the book of private devotions which belonged to John Leche[2] and which we saw containing two offices of the Visitation. Here 'Salutem mentis' (as Suso's office begins) is in a different court hand from that which wrote the offices of the Visitation; there seem to be several hands represented in the book. The office is prefaced: 'Quicumque desiderat eternam sapientam sibi familiarem sponsam habere debet ei has horas devote cotidie legere cum suspirio.' This is not at all the spirit of the 'Sarum' office.

This office ('A solis ortu'), which appears in the Sarum, York, Hereford, and Aberdeen breviaries, is almost certainly an English production, like the mass. It is in prose, in a scriptural and often rhetorical style, particularly in the lessons. Lesson i of the feast refers to the observance of the Transfiguration on the preceding day: 'Heri celebravimus Jesum in celso montis vertice transfiguratum: hodie in ymis terris humilitatem.' Approval of the office is in that lesson ascribed to Alexander IV (pope 1254–61): 'Huius sacratissimi nominis affectu, suave ipsius officium comprobavit, et auctoritate apostolica confirmavit, statuendo diem dulcissimae solemnitatis, septimo ydus Augusti.'[3] In lesson ii indulgences for the observance of the feast are listed, like those which Urban IV (who is named, along

[1] Bodl. MS. Dugdale 47, f. 116.
[2] Trin. Oxf. MS. 13, f. 98.
[3] There is no corroboration for this in *CPL.*

with Martin V and Eugenius IV) authorized for the new feast of Corpus Christi. But these indulgences for the Name of Jesus are only supposed to apply 'per regnum Angliae'.

The lessons are long, and maintain throughout a hortatory tone, as though taken from a sermon. In the full form of the office, as in the printed choir breviaries, the lessons for the octave comprise a thorough anatomy of the name of Jesus. In a typically Western schematization (totally contrary to the Eastern use of the Holy Name in the 'Jesus Prayer' with its aim of emptying the mind) each day on which the octave is observed is devoted to a different aspect of the Name; the second day 'de constitutione', third 'de sanctificatione' (fourth is St. Lawrence), fifth 'de descriptione', sixth 'de praenunciatione' (seventh St. Hippolytus). At one point, in lesson v for the Sunday within the octave, there seems perhaps to be a reference to the sequence 'Dulcis Jesus nazarenus' (or possibly the other way about). Lines 30–4 of the sequence read 'Ignatius hoc docuit / Illud passus insonuit / Cor eius scissum patuit / Inscriptum Jesu coelico'; the lesson is very similar:

> Jesum beatus Ignatius suae passionis in agone invocavit; et bene sibi erat. Bestias ferocissimas, ardentissimos ignes, ac cetera genera tormentorum superavit. Gloriosum memoriale ultra humanam aestimationem corde suo inscriptum suscepit de manu Domini Jesu sempiternum. Namque corde particulatim scisso, litteris aureis inscriptus invenitur Jesus: cuius ob mirabilem gratiam plures venerantur cum fidelis.[1]

The hymns for matins and lauds are centos from 'Jesu dulcis memoria': that for matins is composed of the first five and the ninth and tenth stanzas, according to the earliest numeration;[2] that for lauds is less straightforward, being stanzas thirteen, eighteen, thirty-one, thirty-two, twenty-one, thirty-eight, and thirty-nine. It might be expected that the vespers hymn would also be a cento from the same source, but it is an independent hymn, 'Exultet cor praecordiis', which appears only in English (and Irish) breviaries.[3] It has not been included for any striking

[1] *Legenda Aurea*, 157 (c. xxxvi) contains this story in describing the passion of St. Ignatius.

[2] J. Julian, *A Dictionary of Hymnology* (revised edn., London, 1907), 585, following Bodl. MS. Laud misc. 668.

[3] *RH*, no. 5848; also in Trinity Dublin MS. B. 3. 12, a fifteenth-century 'Sarum' breviary from Trim.

literary merit: 'Nomen sonans suavitur / in metro, prosa, carmine' is an example of the level at which it moves. A proper hymn is also specified for compline, 'Alma chorus domini / nunc pangat nomina summi'. This extraordinary catalogue of Latin, Greek, and Hebrew names which have been applied to Christ (e.g. 'Messias, Sother, Emmanuel, Sabaoth, Adonay / Est Unigenitus, Via, Vita, Manus, Omousyon . . . Agnus, Ovis, Vitulus, Serpens, Aries, Leo, Vermis': it is hard to imagine this being sung with a straight face) appears in manuscripts as early as the tenth and eleventh centuries.[1] It had a number of earlier liturgical uses, generally as a sequence; its customary ending 'Salvaficet nos / sit cui secula / per omnia doxa', is here replaced by 'Nominibus his / Signatur Jesus / Sint Domino laudes'.

Because the cult of the Holy Name was originally centred, liturgically, on a votive mass, and the subsequent transition to the status of a regular feast was by stages, the office appears in only a relatively small number of manuscript service books, and is added to the kalendar in not a great many more. As we have seen, the 'Launton' breviary[2] has a sort of supplement at the back, almost certainly written after 1475, which includes the office of the Holy Name (f. 486). The second of the two offices of the Visitation and the office of the Transfiguration are in one hand which also seems to have written that of the Holy Name; but there is a gap of nearly two blank pages after the Transfiguration, and it is possible that the Name of Jesus was added somewhat later, or that the blank space was intended to contain another office. We have noted other breviaries in which the offices for all three 'nova festa' have been entered.[3] In each case the office for the Holy Name is the same one, 'A solis ortu', and the text is in the various books reasonably uniform.

But there are some notably individual variations in the office included in the sanctorale of a Peterborough (Benedictine) diurnal which has been compiled at different dates.[4] Both the Visitation and the Holy Name have been added to the kalendar, in the same hand, in a blue (it would seem) ink which has now

[1] *RH*, nos. 821–2; *AHMA* liii. 152.

[2] Bodl. MS. Laud misc. 299.

[3] e.g. CUL MSS. Add. 4500, Dd. x. 66 (dated 1435). The office of the Name of Jesus has not been added to the 'Arlingham' breviary (Salisbury Cathedral MS. 152), though it has been inserted in the kalendar.

[4] Bodl. MS. Gough liturg. 17. Van Dijk calls it post 1415; Frere, beginning of sixteenth century; Ker, fourteenth–sixteenth centuries.

faded to a fuzzy grey. The same ink appears sporadically in the sanctorale; this ink, and a slight difference of hand, betray the fact that the two offices have been very cunningly inserted into the original sanctorale. Vespers begins with an antiphon which is not in the Sarum office, 'O bone Jesu spes nostra . . .', under which are included the first four of the five Sarum psalms. The capitulum is also different, 'Omnibus qui invocant . . .' (1 Cor. 1 : 2—the Sarum capitulum at lauds), but the response and versicle which follow are the same as the Sarum. So are the hymn, 'Exultet cor praecordiis', antiphon to the Magnificat, and collect. For the little hours there is only one difference: 'O bone Jesu' is repeated as the antiphon at terce, instead of 'Laudate nomen'. At second vespers in place of the Sarum antiphon, 'Vocatum est', there is the first Sarum antiphon for first vespers, 'A solis ortu', followed by the next three antiphons for first vespers. The response and versicle after the capitulum are new: 'Ecce concipies' and 'Hic erit magnus'. A rubric at the end explains how the feast came to be observed at Peterborough (f. 231^{v}):

Sciendum est quod bone memorie dominus Robertus Kirton [sic] quidam abbas burgi cum consensu totius capituli ordinavit quod festum nominis Jesu celebretur sub more duplici festi et commemoratio de sancto oswaldo ad utriusque vesperas et ad matutinas.

An octave is not indicated. Robert Kirkton was abbot from 1496 to 1528, so we know that the feast was introduced quite late at Peterborough. What the cause of the variations from the Sarum office was we do not know.

One other adaptation—for here the variations from the Sarum office are so extensive as to form almost an entirely new votive office—deserves mention. This is found in a book of miscellaneous offices written for someone who was not a priest, in England, after 1383.[1] In the original hand there are both a nearly complete text (first vespers is lacking) of the office for Richard Rolle[2]—which was compiled while his canonization was being promoted, but which never came into official liturgical use—and also three other offices, including that for the Compassion of the Virgin ascribed to John XXII. Added to these in a different hand is the 'Officium breve per cotidianis

[1] Bodl. MS. e Mus. 193, f. 47^{v}.

[2] Printed in *York Breviary* ii. 785–820.

diebus compilatum in veneratione dulcissimi domini iesu et nominis eius', which, breaking off in the middle of the office of none, concludes the volume. This office, which begins not with vespers but with matins (as does Suso's), has some rhythmical substitutions for prose sections of the Sarum office, and three lessons, which are not the same as any of the usual ones. The hymns are taken from the Sarum office for vespers, 'Exultet cor praecordiis', which is divided in a curious way, the first two stanzas, plus the seventh (which is common to all the hymns) at matins, the fourth and fifth at lauds; for prime and the little hours the first stanza of the usual office hymn is adapted for the occasion—the hymn for terce, for example, begins 'Nunc sancte nobis spiritus / tu cordi nostro imprime / nomen Jesu medullitus / quo cuncta mala comprime'—and another stanza of 'Exultet cor praecordiis' is used to complete the hymn. This is true of at least prime and terce, after which all the stanzas of the hymn in the form we have it have been exhausted; but it is possible that the second halves of the hymn for sext and none are taken from a longer version of 'Exultet cor praecordiis' which we do not possess. It is notable that any use of 'Jesu dulcis memoria' seems to be avoided.

The earliest printed service books show that the Name of Jesus was not yet at their time a generally received feast. Even taking into account that the printed books would tend to be conservative in their texts, we can see how the observance was still, in the 1480s and early 1490s, at the stage of a votive mass (though not accompanied by an indulgence) rather than a liturgical feast. In the 1488 Sarum missal printed at Basel the Holy Name is not in the kalendar, and the mass is placed among the weekly votives, between the Holy Cross and the Five Wounds; but there is in the Bodleian copy a manuscript marginal notation at August 7th in the proper of saints referring the user to the section of votives at the end of the common of saints. The same order is followed in the next editions, printed in Rouen in 1492, and at Venice in 1494; but in the latter case the Name of Jesus has come into the kalendar in red, like the other 'nova festa'. The next step comes in the succeeding edition, Rouen 1497, where the mass is in the sanctorale after the Transfiguration; but there is no rubric dividing the sequence during the octave, and in the copy owned by St. Catherine's

College, Cambridge, the 'divisio' of the sequence has been marked by hand.[1] The first Sarum missal printed in England, London 1498, preserves the same arrangement, and the rubric for observance of the octave only comes with the London and Paris missals of two years later. So it is not until 1500 that the feast achieves its final form in the printed missals.[2]

Despite the fact that the Name of Jesus, along with the Transfiguration, had been officially declared a feast in the province of York in 1489, the first printed York missal, 1509, contains no 'nova festa' in the kalendar, and their masses only in a kind of supplement after the colophon; the sequence at the Jesus mass is not divided. The subsequent editions show no change in these respects. (In the Bodleian copy of the 1517 missal a line has been drawn by hand at the 'divisio' of 'Dulcis Jesus nazarenus'.) The printed Hereford missal (two editions, both printed at Rouen, probably in 1502 and 1510) does not contain the mass of the Name of Jesus at all, nor is the feast included in its kalendar, though the mass had been added to the early fifteenth-century manuscript missal.[3] The Jesus mass was included in the manuscript Arbuthnott missal of 1491, but in a supplement, after the 'Benedictio Salis' and before the 'Gospel of John XXII' and the mass of the Five Wounds.[4] It is not in the kalendar.

The evidence of the early printed Sarum breviaries about the acceptance of the Name of Jesus as a liturgical feast agrees roughly with that of the missals. The only one of the very earliest editions which has survived sufficiently intact for us to be certain that it did not contain the office is the 1483, in which there are no 'nova festa' at all. A separate printing of the office was made probably in 1493, by Pynson at London: the office is 'A solis ortu', with lessons for the octave and with the mass, including the rubric which divides the sequence throughout

[1] It is not absolutely certain that the BM copy and the Cambridge copy represent identical editions, but both were printed at Rouen, probably by M. Morin, and probably in 1497.

[2] From 1500 the two peculiarities which occur in Sarum missals reveal only the idiosyncracies of individual editions. The rubric dividing the sequence is lacking from the editions of 1501 Rouen (Morin), 1504 Paris (Verard), 1508 Paris (Verard), and 1508 Rouen (Morin). The Holy Name is entered in black along with the other 'nova festa' in the 1512 London (Pynson) and the 1520 London (also Pynson) missals.

[3] Univ. Oxf. MS. 78A, f. 226^{v}.

[4] *Arbuthnott Missal*, xcvi.

the octave.[1] The first breviary into which the office is incorporated is the 1494 Paris edition, printed by P. Levet; the feast is also included with the other 'nova festa' in the kalendar. This is the case with most of the succeeding breviaries—1495 Venice, 1496(?) Rouen, and all editions after the turn of the century—but the 1497 Rouen edition reverts to a more conservative arrangement: the Name of Jesus is not in the kalendar, and its office was apparently added in a supplement to the summer part, which is not extant, along with the offices of the Presentation, St. Mary 'ad Nives', St. Osmund, the 'Festum Salvatoris', and St. Chad.[2] The next edition, 1499 Paris, restores the feast to the kalendar, but the office finds a place only at the end of the sanctorale, followed by the office for the Translation of Osmund.[3]

In this breviary, for the first time, a set of mass forms and a series of (presumably) popular masses are provided. This becomes standard in most of the later books, and the Jesus mass is without exception included. But the mass, clearly intended here as a votive (as the others in the series prove: Trinity, Holy Spirit, Holy Cross, Wounds, Blessed Virgin, dead, apostles, and other masses from the common of saints, St. Roch—invoked against plague—'pro febribus', 'pro mortalitate evitanda') always ends with the rubric dividing the sequence during the octave.[4]

The printed York breviaries show the same conservatism as the missals. The first edition, which was printed at Venice in 1493, four years after the Name of Jesus was established by the Northern Convocation, does not include the feast. The next edition, 1507 Rouen, is so defective in its only remaining copy that no information about the Holy Name is educible, and it is not until the third edition, 1526 Paris, that the Name of Jesus appears in both kalendar and sanctorale. The office is 'A solis

[1] Another edition was printed in 1497.

[2] The Bodleian copy is 'Pars Hiemalis', and is the only one known. No 'Pars Estivalis' survives.

[3] This arrangement is occasionally found in later books, perhaps modelled on the 1499, e.g. the 1515(?) Paris.

[4] It is doubtful whether the octave was always observed. Lessons for the octave are omitted in the 1507 London and 1519 Paris editions. But in the 1544 'purged' breviary printed by Grafton and Whitchurch at London the Name of Jesus, which still ranks as a major double, retains its octave, and this is, of course, also true of the Marian editions.

ortu', like the Sarum. This is also true of the two subsequent editions.

In the printed Hereford breviary (1505 Rouen) the feast does not appear in the kalendar but is included in its proper place in the sanctorale,[1] with the rubric, 'Festum maius duplex. Octave cum regimine chori'; but no lessons for the octave are given. The office is again identical with the Sarum. This is also true of the Aberdeen breviary of 1510, but the Name of Jesus is graded in both kalendar and sanctorale as only a minor double. Lessons for the octave are given none the less, with the interesting rubric 'Quotidie infra octavas ubi festum nominis iesu est maius duplex et octave cum regimine chori hoc modo de eisdem octavis fiat servicium': perhaps a recognition of the difference in grading from the Sarum model which Bishop Elphinstone used.[2] The mass of the Holy Name follows immediately after the office.

Printed books besides breviaries and missals bear out the general impression already gained. Hymns (including the compline hymn) and the sequence for the Holy Name were printed in the first Sarum hymnal to include a supplement for new feasts, printed in 1496, probably at London; but they are not included (no 'nova festa' hymns are) in the 1517 York hymnal, the only edition of that book. The 1519–20 Sarum antiphonal, the 1527 gradual, the 1518 legenda, the 1512 diurnal and the 1519 processional—in fact, all the early editions of these supplementary service books—contain the appropriate forms for the Holy Name. The 1490(?) and 1504 editions of the psalter do not contain any 'nova festa' in their kalendars; the changes are made in the third edition, 1506. The Holy Name is always in the kalendar of printed books of hours from what is probably the earliest edition, 1495. In the Paris 1512 Sarum hours it is missing, but since there are only two days in the entire kalendar without a saint, July 3rd and August 7th, it

[1] In contrast with the printed missal, from which the feast is totally absent. In this context it is noteworthy that the Hereford breviary is dedicated to the Lady Margaret, whose devotion to the Holy Name was, as we shall see, well known. The Sarum breviary, 1507 London, was printed expressly for her; only certain parts now survive, including the Jesus mass among the masses.

[2] The lessons in the Aberdeen breviary lack the section which in the Sarum lessons describes the indulgences granted for keeping the feast. The only other notable difference in the lessons of the two breviaries is that the six Sarum lessons for the Sunday within the octave are compassed within three in the Aberdeen book.

looks as though the Visitation, which is in black, was going to be changed to red (though to put it at July 3rd would make it wrong by one day) and the Name of Jesus was going to be added in red. In the 1541 hours printed by Petit of London the feast was called 'the feaste of Jesu'; in the severely pruned kalendar of the 1547 edition (Grafton at London) the Name of Jesus is gone, together with the Visitation and Transfiguration, but all three are restored in the same printer's edition of two years later, and in all subsequent editions. After the extreme conservatism of the other printed York books in admitting the feast, it is surprising to find that the 1517 York hours, printed at Rouen by Cousin, includes the Holy Name in the kalendar before Donatus (the older saint commemorated on August 7th), especially since no other 'nova festa' find a place.[1]

Both Convocations legislated about the new feast roughly when the first printed service books were coming out.[2] At Convocation of Canterbury in 1488 the proctor presented 'quendam quaternum papyri, continentem in se festum de nomine Jesu'; which the archbishop, with the assent of the clergy, then 'statuit et ordinavit fori observandum singulis perpetuis annis futuris, per modum et formam in huius modi quaterno content.'[3] The next year (27 February 1489) Convocation of York established the Name of Jesus for August 7th, as well as the Transfiguration for the preceding day: these changes were in accord with the wishes of the archbishop, Thomas Rotherham.[4] We have seen from Rotherham's will that the establishment of these two feasts was evidently something he wanted to be remembered for.[5] The first part of his will is taken up with provisions for the foundation of a college in his native town of Rotherham, Yorkshire, in honour of the Name of Jesus, to which he had a strong devotion: 'Cuius nomen O si amarem ut deberem et vellem.'[6]

There can be no doubt of the popularity of the cult, and in particular of the Jesus mass, in England.[7] There were Jesus

[1] No 'nova festa' are included in the York processionals of 1530 or even of 1555.

[2] Wordsworth and Littlehales, 193, mentions 'papal sanction' for the Holy Name as well as for the Transfiguration in 1457; this is surely an error.

[3] Wilkins iii. 626, ex Reg. Norton, f. 41.

[4] Reg. Rotherham, Ebor., f. 246, summarized in *Records of Northern Convocation*, 203.

[5] *Testamenta Eboracensia* iv. 138 ff.

[6] Cf. Jesus College, Cambridge, founded by John Alcock, Bishop of Ely, in 1496.

[7] It seems that England led the way in the liturgical celebration of the Holy Name. Of the Roman missals collected by Lippe, the earliest to contain the mass

altars with all the equipment pertaining to them, Jesus guilds which attracted numerous members, and in some cases elaborate ceremonies raising the celebration of the Jesus mass far above the level of an ordinary votive. At Durham there was until the Reformation a 'Jesus altar where Jh'us mess was song every fridaie thorowe out ye whole yere'.[1] This altar stood before the rood screen, and had its own vestments, which were kept in nearby aumbries. On the altar there was a retable which opened to reveal the

> hole Passion of our Lord Jesus christ most richlye and curiously sett furth in most lyvelie coulors all like the burni'ge gold, as he was tormented & as he honge on ye cross wch was a most lamentable sighte to beholde. The wch table was alwaies lockt up but onely on principall daies.

The date of this altar seems not to be known, but since the bodies of two Nevilles who had died in 1367 and 1374 were in 1416 moved from before the Jesus altar to the southern arcade of the nave,[2] it was certainly in existence by the early part of the fifteenth century. In addition to the celebration of the Jesus mass, a special ceremony took place at the altar on Fridays: 'At nyghte after that evinsong was done in ye quier there was an anthem song in ye bodye of ye church before ye foresaid Jh'us alter called Jesus anthem.'[3] We do not know precisely what the text of this anthem was, but it is reasonable to suppose that it may have been what became the antiphon to the Nunc dimittis at compline in the Sarum office, 'O rex gloriose inter sanctos tuos . . .', concluding with the versicle and response 'Sit nomen

is the 1508 edition (*Missale Romanum 1474* ii. 334). The unique copy of the 1482 edition, which shows some English influence in its kalendar (Gilbert of Sempringham, Translation of Thomas of Canterbury), has the Jesus mass added in a manuscript supplement at the end of the book, along with, among others, the masses of the Five Wounds and of the Compassion: A. P. Frutaz, 'Due edizioni rare del "Missale Romanum" pubblicato a Milano nel 1482 e nel 1492', *Miscellanea Giulio Belvediri* (Rome, 1954), 59. A feast of the Holy Name was not papally prescribed until 1721.

[1] *Rites of Durham . . . written 1593* (SS cvii, 1903), 32–5.

[2] *VCH Durham* iii. 118. Later Prior Thomas Castell, who died in 1519, was buried before the Jesus altar (*Rites*, 34); he gave two mills to the cathedral in order to be remembered at the Jesus mass (ibid. 222).

[3] *Rites*, 34. This anthem probably dated from the end of the fifteenth century; the sum of 46*s*. 8*d*. was expended for the Jesus mass and anthem in a sacrist's roll of 1536, but not in the preceding extant roll, 1486–7: *Account Rolls of Durham Abbey* ii (SS c, 1899), 418.

domini Jhesu benedictum; ex hoc nunc et usque in seculum', and with the collect of the mass. Like this anthem, the Friday mass was choral (if not a high mass), for on the north side of the Jesus altar there was a choir loft between two pillars, 'conteyn'ge a paire of orgaines to play on, & a fair desk to lie there bookes on in tyme of dyvin service'.[1]

Thomas Heywood, Dean of Lichfield, established a chantry of Jesus and St. Anne there in 1468, with provisions similar to those at Durham.[2] In addition to a daily mass at the altar (not necessarily of the Holy Name, since a set of vestments was provided for requiems there), a solemn mass of the Name of Jesus was to be sung every Friday at seven o'clock, with six vicars-choral and four choristers assisting. The same complement of singers was also to perform, after compline on Fridays, 'antiphonam devotam et congruentem nomini Yesu, cum versiculis et orationibus pertinentibus': this was to be sung in front of the 'glorious image' of Jesus which was over the altar.[3] An observance after the evening service was also enjoined at the Hungerford chantry in Salisbury cathedral, founded to benefit the soul of Robert, Lord Hungerford, who died in 1459, and his family.[4] The statutes, which were in effect from at least 1472, provide for two chaplains, the first of whom says a different votive mass each day of the week: the Name of Jesus is specified, unusually, for Mondays. At Lincoln there was a Jesus mass with organ only by about 1520; perhaps this was the mass stipulated in the will of Bishop William Smyth, who died in 1514.[5] His will

[1] *Rites*, 34.

[2] J. C. Cox, 'Benefactions of Thomas Heywood, Dean (1457–1492)', *Archaeologia* lii (1890), 617–46. Sixtus IV's bull confirming the chantry in 1479 is translated in *CPL* xiii (i). 264 ff.

[3] According to the chantry returns of Edward VI's reign there was another, and earlier, chantry of the Name of Jesus at Lichfield, founded by Bishop Scrope (1386–98). This was also at the Holy Cross, or Jesus, altar, which was therefore already extant when Heywood founded his chantry (*Gentlemen's Magazine Library: Ecclesiology*, ed. F. A. Milne (London, 1894), 104).

[4] *Ceremonies . . . of Salisbury*, 286. A missal written in the fourteenth century for the Braybroke family (CUL MS. add. 451) contains later obits of the family of Hungerford; the mass of the Holy Name is added in a court hand, without alleluia, sequence, or tract (f. 260v).

[5] H. Bradshaw and C. Wordsworth, eds., *Statutes of Lincoln Cathedral* ii (Cambridge, 1892), p. lxxii. Canon Wordsworth says he does not know whether this involved a special Jesus altar. Smyth's will, printed in R. Churton, *The Lives of William Smyth . . . and Sir Richard Sutton* (Oxford, 1800), 512–20, simply specifies 'coram imagine crucifixi in parte australi dictae ecclesiae existens'.

orders a mass of the Name of Jesus or of the Five Wounds to be said every Friday. He had been translated from Lichfield in 1495, and would consequently have been aware of Heywood's chantry. The Jesus altar of St. Paul's was under the crypt, and there was a guild of Jesus there.[1]

Certainly the Jesus mass was widely known, but this does not mean that the feast was as widely celebrated liturgically, even quite late. We have already remarked its omission at Eton as late as 1517, 'ob defectum librorum'.[2] The Augustinian abbey at Leicester was not observing the feast in 1528: 'Petitur quod possint illud festum habere.'[3] In 1530, the monk-*littérateur* Robert Joseph of Eynsham replied to the request of a friend for 'pagella aliqua', apparently containing antiphons, of the office of the Holy Name; Joseph sends a sheet ('pagina') from the abbot's own copy—this implies an office in loose sheets, rather than added on to a bound book—particularly asking that it should be sent back clean and before the feast-day.[4]

In general, monastic books have forms for the Name of Jesus added to them less often than the secular books. Perhaps there was less opportunity in a monastery for the introduction of a new, popular votive observance (though we have seen it elaborately celebrated at Durham); perhaps some decline in monastic spirituality towards the close of the fifteenth century is a partial explanation. Perhaps also there were fewer new service books in religious houses in the fifteenth century—the surviving evidence tends to bear this out—and later accretions may have been collected in less substantial supplements. One such supplement from the infirmary of St. Albans survives, of about 1500;[5] it includes, as well as some miscellaneous matter, the office and mass for the feasts of Corpus Christi, Oswin (supplanting Phili-

[1] *Documents Illustrating the History of St. Paul's Cathedral* (Camden Soc. N.S. xxvi, 1880), 179, 182.

[2] *Visitations in the Diocese of Lincoln* ii. 137. A marginal insertion in a secular martyrology of the first half of the fifteenth century (Bodl. MS. Bodl. 731, f. 39) reads 'Eodem die festum dulcissimi nominis Jesu cui sit honor'; this book was purchased from one William Menyman in 1489, by Robert Elyot, who had been a fellow of Eton since 1464—an additional proof that awareness of a feast and its observance are by no means the same thing.

[3] Ibid. 189.

[4] *The Letter Book of Robert Joseph* (Oxf. Hist. Soc. N.S. xix, 1967 for 1964), 46. I owe this reference to the kindness of Dr. R. W. Hunt.

[5] St. John's Cbg. MS. 137**.

bert; Oswin's tomb was at Tynemouth, a cell of St. Albans), Anne, and the Eleven Thousand Virgins, and the mass (only) of the Name of Jesus (f. 70^{v}). This means that the Holy Name was not being celebrated as a feast there at the turn of the century. (We have seen that the Peterborough observance was introduced between 1496 and 1528.)

Certainly the office had by no means reached its fullest circulation in, say, the first decade of the sixteenth century, as the Eton 'defectum librorum' shows. Two copies of the office of the Holy Name were sold by the Oxford bookseller John Dorne on 7 August 1520, and two more, bound in parchment, on the 10th of the month when, as Bradshaw points out, services for the octave would be going on.[1] Though no separate copies of the office were printed after 1497, at least that we know of, all the manuscript books still in use would have had, eventually, to be brought up to date; this would have taken time, and have kept the office in circulation.

Bequests from individuals concerning the cult of the Name of Jesus are common at the close of our period, right up until the Reformation changes. Three special chasubles were left to the Jesus altar by a parishioner of Sandwich, Kent, in 1473.[2] Four years later a Somerset man left 6*s.* 8*d.* for the 'Fraternitate Misse Ihu' at Wells.[3] In 1525 John Lord Zouche provided for 'two prestes to synge in the chapell of Jesus by me newe builded in the Priory of Staverdell (Somerset), every Friday they shall say masse de nomine Jesu except Good Friday and the other days masse of the day after the order of the church'.[4] The will of Robert Roose, a farmer or labourer in Yorkshire (probably drawn up, the editor remarks, by the village clergyman 'more suo') in 1520 shows both a determination to be up to date and a most curious grouping of all three principal 'nova festa' under the Holy Name: 'Lego quart. ordii ad emend' festa dulcissimi nominis Jesu, viz. festum Transfigurationis, ac festum

1 H. Bradshaw, *Collected Papers* (Cambridge, 1889), 433. The first was almost certainly an 'officium parvum', and the second was perhaps the same. This could mean either a shorter version of the Sarum office, or Suso's votive office.

2 Scott Robertson, 'St. Mary's Church, Sandwich', *Archaeologia Cantiana* xvi (1885), p. lviii. Other similar examples are cited from the same church.

3 *Somerset Medieval Wills* i (Somerset Record Society xvi, 1901), 354. This was probably at the parish church, St. Cuthbert's, where there was a Jesus chapel at least by 1509: *Soms. Med. Wills* ii. 129.

4 Ibid. i. 244.

dulcissimi nominis Jesu, festumque Visitationis Beate Marie.'[1] Another curious instance is contained in the will of Nicholas Myles (d. 1529) providing money for refreshment in the Hall of Queen's College, Oxford, on his anniversary and on the feast of the Holy Name.[2]

In the last chapter it was noted that, according to Bale, Dr. Henry Horneby, at one time dean of the Lady Margaret's chapel, wrote for her the offices of the Visitation and the Name of Jesus (the latter beginning, he specifies, 'A solis ortu').[3] We are now in a position to review our evidence and to try to say whether that statement can be true, particularly as regards the Holy Name. Nothing in the office gives any indication of a probable date. Whoever composed the Sarum office used, as was customary, the collect from the mass, which was almost certainly in existence by the end of the fourteenth century; and the lessons of the third nocturn comment on the mass gospel.[4] There may, as we have seen, be a reference in the office lessons to the sequence, though this is not certain. The hymns give no clue: all except the vespers hymn are at least three centuries older than the office; and all we know about the vespers hymn is that it was also used by the compiler of the curious votive office referred to earlier.

External evidence is slightly more help. None of the additions of this office to manuscript breviaries must be dated earlier than the 1480s. The office is not in the printed Sarum breviary of 1483 (but none of the 'nova festa' were), was printed separately in 1493, and is included in breviaries from the next year. This might, however, reflect the action of the Convocations in 1488–9 rather than the date the office was actually composed. The feast was introduced at Peterborough after 1496, with an office clearly based on the Sarum; the Plumpton family, as we saw when discussing the Transfiguration, were having an office copied for them in 1498;[5] the 1488 edition of the Sarum Pie has

[1] *Testamenta Eboracensia* v. 116. It is not clear whether he considers all three to be feasts of the Name of Jesus, or only the Transfiguration and Holy Name.

[2] *Liber Obituarius Aulae Reginae in Oxonia* (Oxford Historical Society lvi, 1910), 109.

[3] Bale, *Script.*, pt. ii. 72. He, like Wynkyn de Worde, ascribes Suso's office to Rolle, pt. i. 431.

[4] It is unusual that the capitula, which are taken from different epistles, are totally unconnected with the epistle of the mass, which is from Acts.

[5] *Plumpton Correspondence*, 130.

the entry for August 7th altered to 'de nomine Jhesu, cum octavis cum regimine chori'.[1] A date in the 1480s seems a perfectly likely time for the composition of the office.

It is possible that Horneby was in the Lady Margaret's service, or had at least come under her notice, as early as 1481 when, as we saw, he was given his first living, at East Deeping in Lincolnshire. In 1481 the lordship of Deeping belonged either to the Lady Margaret or to her mother (depending on whether the latter had died by then),[2] so that Horneby may well have begun his career in the pious atmosphere of the Lady Margaret's entourage. Since we do not know his birth date, but only that he became a Master of Arts in 1481 (and died in 1518), we may conjecture that he did not receive the living at younger than the canonical age for priesthood, and that he was consequently mature enough for rather elaborate liturgical composition by at least 1488—assuming that the 'quendam quaternum' presented to Canterbury Convocation was the office favoured by the Lady Margaret.[3] A papal bull of 1494 preserved in the muniments of St. John's College, Cambridge,[4] sanctioning and indulgencing observance of the feast by the Lady Margaret and others, suggests that the office had not been in existence very many years before. An 'officium cum capitulis, lectionibus, antiphonis, versiculis et responsoriis congruentibus' and a 'missa cum eius octava' are mentioned. On balance, it would seem that this office can be equated with the one Bale refers to as having been composed by Horneby, and that the feast, graced by the Lady Margaret's patronage, spread widely in the last decade or so of the fifteenth century.

[1] *Ordinale Sarum, sive Directorium Sacerdotum* ii (HBS xvi, 1902), 659.

[2] I owe the tracing of this possible early connection between Horneby and the Lady Margaret to the late K. B. McFarlane.

[3] That is, if he composed an office for the feast at all. It still seems unlikely that the office of the Visitation can be ascribed to him.

[4] Drawer 56, no. 184; printed in the St. John's magazine, *The Eagle*, xx (1899), 20–1. I am indebted to Mr. A. G. Lee, Librarian of St. John's, for calling my attention to the modern edition.

V

INCIPIENT NEW FEASTS

The Five Wounds

THE popularity of the cult of the Five Wounds during the later middle ages is well known. Like its sister cult of the Holy Name, it had its roots in the 'affective' piety beginning in the twelfth century, and spread by means of private devotions and of a votive mass, the latter enhanced by an impressive if apocryphal legend of authorship and attractive indulgences. In many ways the development of the cult of the Wounds is so much like that of the Holy Name that the point at which they diverge, and the Holy Name attains the character and status of a liturgical feast, is particularly instructive. It is again instructive to see how, in a smaller way, the cult of the Crown of Thorns comes to be observed in England (though to a much lesser degree than on the continent), the only one of a whole series of devotions to the instruments of the passion to obtain any liturgical currency in England. Other such devotions —to the Lance and Nails, for instance, or the Shroud ('Sindon') or Headcloth ('Sudarium')—were probably nipped in England by the Reformation; so it is, in the third place, valuable to see how far these two devotions which did have some circulation in England were accepted.

The mass of the Five Wounds is, in this respect unlike that of the Holy Name, probably an importation into England. Devotions to the Wounds can be found in English manuscripts from the late twelfth century,[1] but not as a part of the liturgical round of mass and office. It has been suggested that the cult of the Five Wounds was first celebrated liturgically in central Europe, at the monastery of Fritzlar in Thuringia;[2] wherever

[1] e.g. Bodl. MS. Tanner 169*, f. 136, a Benedictine psalter from Chester dated 1192–3; and Bodl. MS. Laud lat. 5, f. 9^{v}, an Augustinian psalter from Guisborough (Yorks.) of the late thirteenth century.

[2] L. Gougaud, *Dévotions et pratiques ascétiques du moyen âge* (Paris, 1925), 80.

it began, or at least wherever its mass, 'Humiliavit' (the first word of the introit), was composed, there was a special emphasis on the wound in the side, slightly different from the numerical focus of so many of the English private devotions.

The rubrical legend which generally precedes the Mass of the Five Wounds is very reminiscent of the indulgences to the Jesus mass. Again a pope Boniface is concerned, this time the Second (530–2). The pope, who is mortally ill, appeals to God to prolong his life; the archangel Raphael appears, bearing the text of this mass, which he gives to Boniface with the promise that if he celebrates it five times his health will return. Further benefits are promised for any fivefold celebration: eternal life (with the important hedge 'si in bono perseveret'), relief from any tribulation, and the deliverance from purgatory of souls already dead. Boniface, after conjuring the apparition, and being satisfied of its credentials, adds his apostolic authority, granting—as we have seen in Jesus-mass indulgences—rather more limited benefits than those originally stated: in this case, remission of a seventh part of all sins, and also 'quadraginta dies criminalium et unum annum venialium'. No additional episcopal sanction is supplied.

The context of the mass, then, is clear: a votive mass offering special benefits for performance in a special way, i.e. five times. But it differs from other such mases, like the 'Missa pro mortalitate evitanda',[1] and sets of them, like St. Gregory's Trental, in having a definite subject—the Five Wounds—which links it both with the traditional sequence of daily votive masses, especially that of the Holy Cross, and also with the historical events of Christ's life and passion which, in the cases of the Transfiguration and in an odd way the Name of Jesus,[2] became liturgical feasts.

[1] This mass has a more contemporary historical rubric: 'dominus Papa Clemens fecit et constituit in collegio cum omnibus Cardinalibus . . . cclx dies indulgentiae. Et omnes audientes sequentem Missam debent portare in manu unam candelam ardentem dum Missam audiunt per quinque dies sequentes, et tenere eam in manu per totam Missam, genibus flexis: et eis mors subitanea nocere non potuit. Et hoc est certum et approbatum in Avinione et in partibus circumvicinis' (*Sarum Missal*, 886*). It is often added to English MS. missals, and appears in virtually all printed editions. The mass is commonly called 'Recordare', from the first word of its introit; in the printed Hereford missals it begins 'Reminiscere'.

[2] Which, as the mass gospel makes clear, celebrates in a sense the naming of Jesus.

This double character—a votive observance with the potential of becoming a feast—which we saw clearly with the Name of Jesus, can be seen here in the way the mass of the Wounds is added to English manuscript missals, even though there never comes to be a feast of the Wounds in England, as happens on the continent. The Holy Name and the Five Wounds are often juxtaposed, in contexts which reveal something of the circumstances in which they were received: sometimes among the principal 'nova festa'—Visitation, Transfiguration, Name of Jesus, Wounds, 'Recordare';[1] sometimes after the feasts declared in 1415–16—David, Chad, Winifred, Holy Name, Wounds (in this case without rubric, which also helps define the character of the mass in this situation);[2] sometimes amidst feasts which came in very late in the fifteenth century—Holy Name, Wounds (without legend), 'Recordare', Sebastian, Chrysostom, Gabriel, Antony.[3] The place which the mass comes to have in the printed books, after the Friday votive of the Holy Cross, is anticipated in other manuscript missals or additions to them which seem in general to be later than the first half of the fifteenth century.[4]

The introduction of this mass into England cannot be dated with any precision. The mass of the Wounds was probably not included in English missals quite as early as that of the Name of Jesus. One of the earliest appearances may be in the Sarum missal probably written for the Durham monks in the first half of the fifteenth century.[5] This missal has in what appears to be the original hand the votives of 'Salus populi', the Holy Name, the Wounds, and 'Recordare', each of the last three being preceded by explanatory rubrics. The legend for the Wounds in this missal is of particular interest (f. 233^{v}): 'Sequitur devotissima quinque plagarum christi missa facta(?) a sancto iohanne evangelista omni die dicenda et praecipue in feria sexta cui papa (blank space) duodecimus concessit tam dicentibus quam

[1] Bodl. MS. Hatton 1, f. 221^{v}; CUL MS. Gg. v. 24, f. 297, ends Visitation, Transfiguration, Holy Name, Wounds, and 'pro sponsalibus'.

[2] Bodl. MS. Barlow 5, f. 271; cf. the Irish (Sarum) missal, Lambeth MS. 213, f. 233: Finian, David, Chad, Holy Name, Wounds, 'Pro rege', 'Recordare'.

[3] Gonville and Caius Cbg. MS. 146 (196).

[4] e.g. All Souls Oxf. MS. 11 (end of fifteenth century); cf. BM MS. Egerton 2677, where the Holy Name and Wounds are added at the end of the Temporale, and followed by the normal Saturday votives of the Virgin.

[5] Bodl. MS. Laud misc. 302.

audientibus cc dies indulgentiae tociens quociens dicta vel audita fuerit(?).' Note that the word for 'wound' is 'plaga' rather than 'vulnus', as in almost all other English missals; that the mass is ascribed initially to St. John the Evangelist, and neither Pope Boniface nor the archangel Raphael is mentioned; that though the mass can be said on any day, Friday is specified —which came to be the usual day in the sequence of votive masses; and that the name of the pope has been left blank (not scratched out), but his number, the twelfth, is given. The only popes to whom this could have applied are the scandalous John XII (955–64), Benedict XII (1334–42),[1] or Gregory XII (1406–15). Why should the pope's number be given but not his name? The answer may of course lie in the text from which the scribe copied, but it may also be conceivable that Gregory's name was intended (which would help to date the missal) but that the scribe, learning of his resignation, decided to omit it and subsitute the name of another pope 'the twelfth'.

The text of the mass, too, shows its double character. As would be expected, most of the chant texts are also found in masses of Passiontide;[2] the prayers, which are peculiar to this mass, have the same, general, Passiontide character. It is doubtful whether they were composed as a set. The post-communion reads like a prayer at sext in a votive office, and indeed is very similar to the prayer ascribed to Alcuin.[3] The collect, which is more verbose and is ramblingly constructed, looks to have been composed by someone who already knew the post-communion, for it is essentially a longer version of the same idea, and indeed the two prayers share verbatim the phrase 'et sanguinem tuum pretiosum in remissionem peccatorum nostrorum (ef)fudisti' but the collect is specifically about the Five Wounds, 'et in ligno crucis quinque plagas sustinuisti'. The secret, while mentioning the 'lignum crucis', is concerned with the theme of light, and seems unconnected to the other two; neither it nor the

[1] No such indulgence seems to have been issued by Benedict XII; at least it is not in his register, ed. in the *Bibliothèque des Écoles Françaises d'Athènes et de Rome*, 3rd ser., no. 2 (3 vols., 1902–11), and no. 9 (3 vols., 1898–1920).

[2] Whoever composed the mass used the Vulgate text for the introit, Phil. 2:8 ('Humiliavit semetipsum') rather than following the version of Phil. 2:8 which had been employed in the two other missal uses of this text, at the masses of Holy Thursday and of the Cross. This is also true of the Roman missals of both 1474 and 1570, which share essentially the Sarum text for the mass of the Wounds.

[3] *PL* ci. 463.

post-communion contains any eucharistic reference, which raises further suspicions that they were not originally mass prayers. Emphasis on the wound in the side is found in the lessons, both of which are unique to this mass. For the epistle, verses from Zechariah 12 and 13 are used: '. . . et aspicient in eum quem confixerunt . . .' The gospel focuses entirely on the side wound (John 19 : 28–35): 'Sed unum militum lancea latus ejus aperuit, et continuo exivit sanguis et aqua.' This is also true of the only non-Biblical chant,[1] the offertory, which rehearses indignities of the Passion rather in the style of the Tenebrae responds: 'Insurrexerunt in me testes iniqui: absque misericordia quaesierunt me interficere: et non pepercerunt in faciem meam spuere et lanceis suis vulneraverunt me, et concussa sunt omnia ossa mea.' The most commonly used sequence for the mass, 'Coenam cum discipulis', would more reasonably fit a mass of the one wound in the side than of the five wounds. It is a long composition; the Passion story is paraphrased for fifty-two lines, after which there are three points: a stanza of self-deprecation in the first person singular (e.g. 'Ego pomum mordeo, tu felle potaris'); two stanzas specifically about the lance wound, from the standpoint of the Virgin's reaction; and two stanzas of exhortation to the sinner, the second in the imperative singular. It is not one of the masterpieces of medieval Latin hymnody.

The sequence is the only element of any considerable variation in English texts of the mass.[2] At least four alternative sequences are to be found in English books. The first is an imitation, or alternatively an improved version, of 'Coenam cum discipulis', beginning 'Cenam salutiferam'.[3] The only appearance which is known is in the British Museum copy of the 1504 printed Sarum Missal (Pynson, London), in which a highly defective text of the mass of the Five Wounds ends with only the first three letters, 'Cen-', of the sequence printed; the remainder is added in manuscript, beginning with the completion of the first word, '-ā salutiferā salvator curavit'. The two

[1] Except for the Alleluia.

[2] The one exception to this is in the Durham missal with the unusual rubric (Bodl. MS. Laud misc. 302), where the secret is 'Oblatum tibi domine sacrificium intercedente unigeniti filii tui domini nostri jesu christi passione vivificet nos semper et muniat': obviously a genuine secret, and the one which appears in the Roman missals.

[3] *AHMA* xl. 35–6.

have many expressions, even whole lines, in common, and their structures are basically the same, though 'Cenam salutiferam' omits the first-person apology and addresses the Virgin directly after describing her sorrows: 'Per haec dei vulnera / virgo, tui nati / Aeque nos fac animo / hic adversa pati.' Certainly the imitation is more polished Latin.

The other three sequences are totally independent of 'Coenam cum discipulis'. One appears in two manuscripts,[1] 'Plangat Syon salvatorem'. Again it is largely concerned with a somewhat rhetorical paraphrase of events of the trial and crucifixion. Again, too, the role of the Virgin is stressed: 'Virgo compar passionis', 'Virgo mater dolorata'; 'Peccatorum medicina'.[2] The most extraordinary thing in the sequence is a stanza about the Virgin which contains six Hebrew letters: 'Virgo, mater Christi Iesu, / Scribitur in threnis vau, / Iod, heth, teth(?), lamed, tau / Moysi pentatico.' This extraordinary garble may be an attempt to spell out the Hebrew word 'B(e)thul(a)h' (virgin), while the reference 'in threnis' is almost surely a mistake for S. of S. 2: 1–2, which would help to make slightly more sense of the lines immediately preceding this stanza: 'Ut in threnis Jeremiae / Languet rosa lilio.'[3] 'Moysi pentatico' seems nonsense.

The sequence 'Redemptorem veneremur' is found in a late fifteenth-century Sarum missal which does not contain the rubric for the mass.[4] It is much more straightforward than any of the sequences we have considered. Its standpoint is that of a worshipper looking at an image of the crucifixion: 'Redemptorem veneremur / in cruce pendentem / De suis vulneribus / sanguinem fundentem'; and it is essentially meditation rather than narration. The fifth sequence to be found in English missals, 'Ista sunt praecipue', is, like the preceding one, known in only a single manuscript,[5] and is also relatively brief and

[1] Bodl. MS. Barlow 1, f. 434 (the Gawsworth, Cheshire missal, fifteenth century), and BM MS. Add. 24198, f. 126, a fourteenth-century Irish Augustinian collectar with some later additions for St. Thomas's church in Dublin. Text in *AHMA* xl. 33–4.

[2] This tendency culminates, of course, in the cult of the Compassion of the Virgin, to be treated presently.

[3] The two MSS. have slightly different transliterations of these letters. I am indebted to the Revd. Dr. H. F. D. Sparks for suggesting how this tangle of letters might make sense.

[4] All Souls Oxf. MS. 11. Text in *AHMA* xlii. 24–5.

[5] BM MS. Eg. 2677. Text in *AHMA* xxxvii. 27–8. The legend to the mass is interesting in that it specifies Boniface VIII (1294–1303) as the sick pope.

unrhetorical. Its general pattern is that the first half of each stanza recites an indignity suffered by the Lord, while the second half contains an 'ut' clause showing the benefits therefrom. The somewhat bland tone of the verse is shown by the first and last lines: 'Ista sunt praecipue / Nobis recolenda / Iesu clementissime, / Sive memoranda . . . Haec nos sancta vulnera / Quinque memorata / Possidere gaudia / Faciant beata.'

The sequence in the printed York missals is a curious combination of 'Coenam cum discipulis' with the end of 'Redemptorem veneremur'. The entire text of the first is given,[1] with the last four stanzas of the second added at the end. This conflation may show that 'Redemptorem veneremur' was more widely known, and by 1493, than the sole missal in which it is found would indicate. It is hard to imagine why anyone would wish to add to the already excessive length of 'Coenam cum discipulis'.

Printed Sarum missals from the earliest editions contain the mass of the Five Wounds with its rubric. Its location is almost invariably among the votive masses, after those of the Cross and the Name of Jesus (until the latter is moved into the sanctorale) and before that of the Crown of Thorns. The sole exception is in the 1494 Venice edition, where the mass 'Pro infirmis' is inserted between the Jesus mass and 'Humiliavit'. In the 1510 Paris edition the mass is listed in the contents as an alternative to the Holy Cross for Fridays in the rota 'Misse dicende per ebdomadam'. This could be said to be the highest point the cult of the Wounds ever reached liturgically in England; it remained a votive, to be used at the choice of the priest or the mass-donor at will and when no other mass was prescribed.[2] As far as we know, a Feast of the Five Wounds was never celebrated in England as it came to be on the continent, and none of the rhythmical offices composed for it was used in England. The mass appeared in printed Sarum breviaries from the first edition which contains a selection of masses (Paris, 1499). In the

[1] The penultimate stanza in the Sarum text, 'Fundunt rivos sanguinis', is placed after the stanza describing the actual crucifixion, rather than after the piercing; the effect is to lessen emphasis on the side wound. The York order is followed in J. Kehrein, *Lateinische Sequenzen des Mittelalters* (Mainz, 1873), 63–5.

[2] The statutes of the Hungerford chantry at Salisbury, giving rules for observance there from at least 1472, stipulate, as we saw in the last chapter, a different votive mass for each day of the week: that for Friday was the Five Wounds (*Ceremonies . . . of Salisbury*, 286).

breviaries it was placed between masses of the Cross and of the Virgin, and, more important, was deprived of its legend. For this reason, presumably, it was not excised in the 'purged' 1541 breviary printed by Whitchurch. It is doubtful whether the mass was ever sung, as some votive masses were; in the two editions of the Sarum gradual of 1527 and 1532 music is given for some votive masses but not for the Wounds.

In other English uses its fortunes were about the same. In all the printed York missals the mass appears at the end of the temporale, before the dedication of the church, rather than in the supplement after the sanctorale with the 'nova festa' and the Crown of Thorns. The printed Hereford missals do not contain the mass, though it was added to a manuscript missal.[1] The Arbuthnott missal has the mass added, next to the Jesus mass.[2] There are slight differences from the Sarum form: the legend is somewhat shorter, and the angel who comes to Boniface is Michael, not Raphael; the collect lacks one phrase of the Sarum collect, and is therefore identical with that in the masses appearing in printed Roman missals from 1505.[3]

The Crown of Thorns

The mass of the Crown of Thorns ('Corona Domini') stands, as we have intimated, in roughly the same relation to the Five Wounds as does the Five Wounds to the Name of Jesus. It is certainly very late in arriving in England from the continent. It appears in all printed Sarum missals, always as a votive, always following the Five Wounds; it is also to be found in the printed York, but not Hereford, missals. But even though its position makes clear that it is only an optional votive mass, with special appropriateness to Friday, but with probably lesser claims than the masses of the Cross and the Wounds, there are indications that it, too, was at the very beginning of the process of becoming a liturgical feast in the early years of the sixteenth century, as it had been a feast long before in some places on the continent.

The continental influence is plain in the text of the mass, particularly in the sequence: in fact the mass is almost certainly

[1] Univ. Oxf. MS. 78A, f. 225. [2] *Arbuthnott Missal*, c–cii.

[3] *Missale Romanum 1474* ii. 330. The printed Roman missals, however, include no sequence.

that composed to commemorate the reception of the Crown of Thorns at Paris by St. Louis in 1239. The introit uses the 'Gaudeamus omnes' formula which is appropriate to a feast, not a votive: '. . . diem festum celebrantes sub honore coronae Domini'; and it is clear from the collect that the crown which is the focus of the mass is an actual relic ('coronam ejus spineam veneramur in terris'). The sequence, 'Si vis vere gloriari',[1] expands and corroborates:

Jocunda mysteria
sunt haec, sed materia
praesentis laetitiae,
Nobis est historia
qua patentur Francia
coronatur hodie.
Huius coronatio
coronae susceptio
cujus festum agimus;
Debito cum gaudio
et anniversario
honore recolimus.

A few stanzas later, the sequence launches into an encomium of France and especially of Paris:

Tria privilegia
regna tibi alia
subdunt in honore;
Fides et militia
unctioque regia,
quarum flores flore;
Tibi, O urbs inclyta,
omni laude praedita,
mater studiorum,
Est corona tradita,
et in te reposita,
urbs Parisiorum.

It is not easy to believe that this text would have been very cheerfully sung in England; and since, as in the case of the

[1] *RH*, no. 18910; *AHMA* viii. 21. It is also given in de Riant, *Exuviae Sacrae Constantinopolitanae* ii. 47, under the heading 'In festo Susceptione Sanctae Coronae 11 Aug.'.

Wounds, the mass does not appear in the two printed Sarum graduals of 1527 and 1532, the sequence probably never rose above an inaudible mumble on early Tudor lips. There is no rubric or legend to this mass: a further indication of its historical rather than apocryphal origin.

Until we can know more about what texts the early printers worked from in issuing their editions of service books, we cannot say with much exactness how an observance like that of the Crown of Thorns got into English circulation. It is generally clear from private devotions and manuscript illuminations that the cult of the Instruments of the Passion was popular in England during the fifteenth century; but what is needed is a concrete explanation of why the cult of the Corona should have been the only one to receive liturgical expression in England, and why its mass is largely confined in England to printed books, and consequently to a date from about 1490. Manuscript mentions are very few. The most interesting is in a Sarum psalter and collection of masses[1] which belonged to Oliver Whetenal, vicar of Besthorpe in Norfolk from 1445 to 1469; the psalter is in one hand and common votive masses are in a second; a third has added a kyrie, and in a fourth there are the masses 'Recordare', St. Winifred, and 'In festo coronae domini'. The mass has two striking variations from the usual text: there is no sequence, and the introit is 'omnes gentes plaudite'; that is, the two most explicit references to the mass as a feast have been removed, and it is now a perfectly unremarkable votive mass—despite its title, 'in festo'. There is, of course, no indication that the mass was added during Whetenal's ownership.

By the sixteenth century there was a certain awareness in England that a feast of the Crown of Thorns was observed in some places on the continent. The most obvious example is Richard Whitford's addition to the Syon martyrology for August 11th, in his *Martiloge* of 1526:

The feest also of the crowne of our sauyour / the one halfe wherof Charlemayne brought from constaninople unto parys / at ye departure et divisyon wherof ye same crowne flourysshed & brought forth grene leves and fresshe floures / of the wuiche leves & floures the sayde king charles fylled both his glouves / & reserved them for relykes. And of the people yt were present .ccc. & mor were heled

[1] Bodl. MS. Don. d. 85, f. 103v.

of dyverse sekenes by ye odour & smell that came therfrom wt many other grete miracles.[1]

Now, the date most frequently observed for the 'Susceptio Coronae', as it was originally called, is May 4th, which was kept by the Dominicans in the thirteenth century,[2] at many places in Germany,[3] and by the early sixteenth century at Uppsala and Lund.[4] But at Paris August 11th was observed, as Whitford states. This date does not appear in the kalendar of English service books; but the fact that it was known in England, and that the votive mass in the English books is that of the feast in Paris, makes it clear that the potential feast of the Crown of Thorns in England was modelled on the French feast. In the printed English missals the mass is invariably headed 'in festo Coronae Domini': a heading virtually unique among votives.[5]

Two religious orders had a special interest in the feast of the Crown of Thorns. We have just seen that the Dominicans kept an observance from the thirteenth century, at least in some places. In a breviary with missal additions of the thirteenth and fourteenth centuries,[6] an office of the 'Corona Domini' is in the original hand (f. 292), while the mass has been added (f. 252) by the same hand which added masses of Peter Martyr and Dominic. The office is a rhythmical composition beginning 'Assunt dominici serti sollempnia', with three lessons. (This office will be discussed shortly.) It is not certain that this is an English book. A number of later Dominican and English saints have been inserted into the fourteenth century kalendar—and also the Transfiguration, Visitation, and 'Corona' at May 4th —but there are some additional offices or lessons for Low Countries saints as well. Not enough English Dominican service books survive to make comparison possible.

The same lack of evidence applies to the Cistercians. In a Buckland kalendar and consuetudinary of the fourteenth cen-

[1] *The Martiloge in Englysshe after the Use of the Chirche of Salisbury and as it is Redde in Syon, with Addicyons* (HBS iii, 1893), 126.

[2] Bonniwell, *Dominican Liturgy*, 104. Louis had sent two Dominicans to bring the relic back from the Emperor Baldwin II.

[3] Grotefend, *Zeitrechnung* ii (ii), 88.

[4] A. A. King, *Liturgies of the Past* (London, 1959), 408.

[5] The only exception is the mass found in the 1498 Sarum missal, 'in festo Sancti Armagili'.

[6] BM MS. Roy. 2. A. xi.

tury,[1] the kalendar entry at August 11th reads 'Spinee corone xii lc.' in red, before Tiburtius. The directions in the consuetudinary for that day specify (f. 87) 'Maior autem missa erit de corona domini ad quam dicetur credo sed cum nulla speciale prefacione', and refer to the Cistercian General Chapter of 1242. At that Chapter the feast of the Crown of Thorns, previously observed by the French abbeys, was extended to the entire order.[2]

It was said that the mass of the Crown of Thorns is included in all editions of the printed Sarum missals, following the Five Wounds, and that it appeared in York but not Hereford missals. In the printed York missals, where the mass of the Wounds is inserted after the temporale, the Corona follows the three principal 'nova festa' in the supplement at the end of the book. Except in the relatively small area covered by the use of Hereford, therefore, the mass of the Crown of Thorns was known all over England by 1500. It was not added to the Arbuthnott Missal of 1491 as were the Holy Name and the Wounds, both in the scribe's hand: this is perhaps another fact pointing to the spread of its popularity some time in the 1490s (the first printed Sarum missals date from about four years before the Arbuthnott was written). There is no office in the breviaries of any of these uses: but in a supplement to the Aberdeen breviary printed around 1520, ten years after the main text, there are given offices for the Compassion of the Virgin, the Crown of Thorns, and the coming of the relics of St. Andrew into Scotland.[3] This office, which has some curious features, offers an indication, and an important one, of how this observance would have become a feast.

The date is specified in a rubric: 'In die inventionis sanctae crucis ad secundas vesperas fiat solemnis memoria de corona domini', i.e. a solemn memorial in place of first vespers on May 3rd, and the feast on May 4th. At the memorial an antiphon with versicle and response, and a collect, the same as at the mass, are given; the office itself begins with the invitatory at matins 'Assunt dominici serti solennia, laude multiplici plaudat

[1] BM MS. Harl. 2931.

[2] *Statuta Capitulorum Generalium Ordinis Cisterciensis 1116–1786*, ed. J. M. Canivez, ii (Louvain, 1934), 245.

[3] Text in Preface to 1854 edn. of *Aberdeen Breviary*, printed separately; no pagination. For St. Andrew's relics only nine lessons are given.

ecclesia: alleluya', and the hymn 'Eterno regi gloriae'. There are three lessons, with rhythmical responsories. The whole office seems to be a shortened form of a rhythmical office 'Gaude felix mater ecclesia',[1] which has been traced to a fifteenth-century Swedish legenda and to the Linkoeping breviary of 1493.[2] Important differences between the Linkoeping and Aberdeen texts prove that the latter was not a verbatim copy. The antiphons at the memorial in place of first vespers differ, and the Aberdeen office has only three psalms at matins, and consequently only three antiphons. The Swedish office has a third hymn, for second vespers, 'Corona filia Syon'. The first lessons in the two are substantially the same; they also agree, up to a point, with the beginning of the chapter added to the *Legenda Aurea*, 'De corona domini nostri Jesu Christi'.[3] At the end of the lesson, the chapter in the *Legenda* continues 'ideo aeterno regi gloriae . . .' and goes on to give, though not printed as verse, the four stanzas (excluding doxology) of the matins hymn of that name in both offices. Both offices also agree, against the *Legenda*, in reading 'recolligimus salutis nostre messem' instead of 'recolimus salutem nostrae animae', in the first lesson. But after the first lesson the Aberdeen office and *Legenda* agree substantially, while the second and third lessons of the Swedish office differ totally from the other two. The response at the end of Aberdeen lesson ii, rhythmical though it is, is printed continuously with the rest of the text in the *Legenda*, like the matins hymn above. The same is true of the response to lesson iii, and the *Legenda* chapter closes with the phrases used as the antiphon to the Magnificat at second vespers in both Aberdeen and Linkoeping offices.

These variations suggest the existence of another rhythmical office from which both the Aberdeen and the Linkoeping versions were taken, and also the account in the *Legenda Aurea*, which incorporates both a hymn and some of the rhythmical matter as well as lesson material, and must therefore have been taken from a complete office. Perhaps it was an office of nine lessons, of which the Aberdeen and Linkoeping books have

[1] *RH*, no. 6789; *AHMA* xlv. 16–18. The same is true of the office in the Dominican breviary which was discussed earlier, the provenance of which is not certain.

[2] *Breviarium Lincopense*, ed. K. Peters et al. (Lund, 1950–8), 645 ff.

[3] p. 955 (cap. ccxlii).

between them five. Though the lessons are not taken from two of the more probable sources, the Paris office[1] or the Norwegian office of the *Breviarium Nidrosiense*,[2] a fourteenth-century breviary from Clermont (where there was a relic of the Thorns from 1269) contains an office including the two hymns shared by the Aberdeen and Linkoeping offices,[3] so it is possible that a common source, including hymns, rhythmical parts, and offices, may have existed.

At any rate, the printing of the office in the supplement to the Aberdeen breviary shows that a feast of the Crown of Thorns was to be celebrated somewhere in Scotland in 1520,[4] almost certainly as a result of continental, perhaps Scandinavian, influences. Because there was no later printed Scottish missal, we do not know whether the mass was introduced to complement the office on May 4th. For England, there is only one real indication that a new feast of the Crown of Thorns was even incipient, and that is very late. The printed Sarum hours of 1551 (Rouen), 1554 (London), and 1557 (London) include in their kalendars the Corona Domini on May 4th. These three contain a saint for each day, so this evidence (particularly since the date is not the one which was celebrated at Paris, and which the 'Sarum' mass would lead one to expect) cannot be accorded very much significance.

The Compassion of the Virgin

The extent of liturgical celebration of the Virgin's Compassion in later medieval England can be simply stated. In the printed Sarum missal of 1497 (Rouen) there appears, among the supplementary masses at the end and between those of Gabriel and Barbara, the 'Missa Compassionis sive Lamentationis B. Mariae'. It is included in about half the subsequent editions until 1526, after which it is in all the editions until the very last, London, 1557.

1 Printed in de Riant, *Exuviae* ii. 38 ff. and i. 45–8 and 55–6.

2 Ibid. i. 4–6 (a piece of the Crown of Thorns had been brought to Norway in 1273).

3 F. de Mely, *Exuviae Sacrae Constantinopolitanae* (Paris, 1904; a continuation of de Riant's 2 vols.), 312. They are also found in thirteenth-century Dominican offices: *AHMA* lii. 13.

4 Not much is known about the supplement to the *Aberdeen Breviary*; only one copy exists and there is no way of telling how many copies were printed, or how widespread was its influence.

The mass which, as we shall see, is not English in origin, is an interesting example of liturgical composition, and justifies some detailed attention. The first thing to notice is a paradoxical characteristic of a number of late, originally votive masses, seen in this mass to an exaggerated degree: the contrast between the brevity of the gospel (John 19:25–7) and the length of the sequence, 'Moesta parentis Christi'. This sequence has the same rhetorical, long-winded quality as those of the Five Wounds and the Corona; but as a piece of rhetoric it is of considerable effect. As in other sequences, there are several shifts in person as the stanzas progress: it begins in the third person, switches to the first with rather striking irony ('Est ista-ne gratia, quam sic mihi retulisti, Gabriel, dicens Ave Maria, gratia plena?'), and returns to the third person to describe what could easily be a fifteenth-century Pietà: 'O lacrymosa intuita, sedet semimortua parens et extincti funeris in gremio tenet exuvias. / Omnia pererrat stigmata locaque cruenta clavorum necnon et plagas singulas . . .'. As the burial preparations are described the point of view becomes one of devout commentary, and the words grow strongly reminiscent of the 'Stabat Mater': 'Quis potest lacrymas tenere licet corde saxeo, et non simul condolere in hoc planctu virgineo?' A series of Old Testament parallels is then introduced—Hannah, Rachel, Naomi, Anna the mother of Tobit—and the sequence closes with an appeal to the Virgin which is again close to that of the 'Stabat Mater' (which, incidentally, does not seem to have been used in medieval England)[1]: 'Sic, O virgo dolorosa, fac nos tecum lacrymosa sentire suspiria: / ut post vitam infelicem habeamus te ductricem ad aeterna gaudia.' Following this rather elaborate composition the brief gospel seems somewhat incongruous, and one is tempted to think that, as in the case of the Wounds and the Crown of Thorns, the sequence was generally read to himself by the celebrant at this votive mass.[2]

[1] The printed York missals, and also the manuscript missal Univ. Oxf. 78B, contain a sequence, 'Stabat juxta Christi crucem', for commemoration of the Virgin on Fridays (so the rubric reads, though Saturday was more usual) between Trinity and Advent. This sequence seems the closest thing to the 'Stabat Mater' in England. Text in *York Missal* ii. 209, and *AHMA* viii. 56; *RH*, no. 19412 suggests a fourteenth-century origin.

[2] But in D. McRoberts, *Catalogue of Scottish Medieval Liturgical Books and Fragments* (Glasgow, 1953) there is noted (no. 43, p. 9) a fragment of a fifteenth-century

Also noteworthy, though not surprising, is the extensive use of the Lamentations of Jeremiah: as both introit ('Vide, Domine, quoniam tribulor') and psalm-verse, for the epistle (2 : 13, 15–19), beginning of the gradual (which continues with Ruth 1: 20: was this perhaps suggested by the reference to Naomi in the sequence, which could have been composed independently—or the other way round?), and both the alternate alleluyas for Easter-tide. Only in the tract are the Psalms employed, a cento skilfully compiled from three different psalms. The remaining chants, offertory, and communio, are in verse, and seem to be snatches from a longer rhythmical office.[1] The prayers are proper to the mass; the collect commences 'Pietatem tuam'—the mass is sometimes alternatively called 'de Pietate'[2]—and concludes with a request to share in the eternal felicity of both Christ and his mother ('vobiscum'). The preface is of the Cross, 'Qui salutem'.

Several years before the first English missal to contain the mass of the Compassion, Caxton printed at Westminster a 'Commemoracio lamentacionis sive compassionis beate Marie in morte filii . . . quam celebrari debet feria sexta immediate procedente dominica in passione . . .'. Only one edition was printed, and the sole surviving copy is in the University Library of Ghent.[3] The office is not incorporated into any English breviaries, and the only other indication that a feast of the Compassion was even incipient is in the same supplement to the Aberdeen breviary, printed about 1520, which we saw containing the office of the Crown of Thorns. Here the rubric reads 'In festa dolorose compassionis beate Marie. quod celebratur annuatim feria quarto post dominicam in ramis palmarum'—that is, Wednesday of Holy Week. The office, which is rhythical, begins 'Omnis etas defleat' at first vespers, and the invitatory at matins starts 'Cum Maria virgine fervide ploremus'.

The Compassion of the Virgin at the Crucifixion, and indeed

gradual, now at Stirling, which contains the sung parts of the votive mass of the Compassion. The mass does not appear in English graduals, MS. or printed.

[1] In *AHMA* xlix. 330 and 360 they are traced only to a Langres missal of 1549.

[2] There was an altar of Our Lady of Pity in the nave at Durham: *VCH Durham* iii. 118.

[3] E. G. Duff, *Fifteenth Century English Printed Books* (Oxford, 1917), 30 gives the date as 1490; Bradshaw, *Sarum Breviary* iii, p. lii dates the office at 1487. Excerpts are given in M.-L. Polain, *Catalogue des livres imprimés au quinzième siècle des Bibliothèques de Belgique* i (Brussels, 1932), 728–9.

her sorrows in general, as reflected in the 'Sorrowful Mysteries' of the Rosary, provided one of the most popular subjects of late medieval devotion. But it is not late medieval exclusively: Wilmart has shown how in the late eleventh and early twelfth centuries special attention was paid to Mary at the foot of the Cross.[1] The more tender, 'affective' piety which we have noticed in connection with the cults of the Holy Name and the Instruments of the Passion extended also to the life of the Virgin. As we shall see, interest in the infancy of Jesus is mirrored in stories of the Virgin's early life, evident both in the cult of her Presentation and in that of her mother, St. Anne. Likewise, Christ's Passion is made to have a parallel in the sufferings of his mother.[2] It is, therefore, natural that liturgical and private devotions concerning the Passion should be imitated for the Compassion of the Virgin. Bonaventure's well-known rhythmical office, 'In passione Domini', is thus the model for the office which begins 'Cum maria virgine fervide ploremus'—of which the Aberdeen office is a considerably expanded version. 'Cum Maria' was in the middle ages ascribed to both Bonaventure[3] and John XXII,[4] and enjoyed considerable popularity from the late fourteenth century (the date of its earliest manuscripts). Versions of it can be found in several English manuscripts of private devotions.[5]

While the Compassion was the subject initially of private devotion, it began also to be observed liturgically from the early fifteenth century. The Council of Cologne in 1423 instituted for the Friday after Easter III a 'Festum commemorationis praefatae angustiae et doloris B.M.V.', partly in reparation for Hussite sacrileges against images of the Virgin.[6] This would have been purely a local feast, and, as its name implies, concentrates on only one of Mary's sorrows, i.e. at the Crucifixion. Mary's agony at the foot of the Cross, including her part in the burial preparations, is the climax of her Compassion, and the

[1] *Auteurs Spirituels*, 505–36: 'Prières de Compassion'.

[2] E. Mâle, *L'art religieux de la fin du moyen âge en France* (Paris, 1908), 118–40.

[3] The authenticity and manuscripts of this office are discussed in the Quaracchi edition of Bonaventure's works, viii (1898), p. cvii. 'In passione domini' is printed in the same vol., p. 151. 'Cum maria virgine' is included in the Vatican edition of Bonaventure, vi (1596), 485 ff.

[4] Discussed by N. Valois in *Histoire littéraire de la France* xxxiv (Paris, 1914), 534.

[5] Bodl. MSS. e Mus. 193, f. 34, and Rawl. C. 558, f. 135; BM MS. Cott. Faust. A. vi, f. 158.

[6] Mansi xxviii. 1057.

emphasis of the Cologne feast is therefore the natural outcome of the earlier devotions noted by Wilmart. Though the feast of the Seven Sorrows, as such, was only promulgated in 1668 (to commemorate the foundation of the Servites; celebrated on September 15th), it is now clear that the enumeration of Mary's sorrows in a devotional context dates from as far back as the early fourteenth century,[1] and not from the ardours of Flemish —or more accurately, Burgundian court—spirituality at the very end of the fifteenth and beginning of the sixteenth centuries as Delehaye had argued.[2]

The importance for our purposes of the small controversy on this point is that it suggests a two-fold influence which may have been felt in England: the general current of devotion which was increasingly concerned with the Compassion of the Virgin; and the specific impetus of the founding of the confraternity of the Seven Sorrows, under the patronage of Philip the Fair of Burgundy and shortly with papal approval, in 1492.[3] The first may be seen in the appearance of the office 'Cum Maria virgine' in English books of private devotion, as we have already noticed, and in the Caxton edition of another office. The second may be significantly reflected in the date of the first English missal to contain the 'Missa Compassionis', 1497. Certainly there was a mass of the Compassion well before this date; by the end of the fifteenth century there was more than one. Among the four different masses having to do with the Compassion which appeared in printed Roman missals before 1570[4] there is not only the mass of the Sarum missals but also a 'Missa nostre domine pietatis per papam sixtum quartum edita', which begins 'Cumque vidisset' and is almost entirely different from the mass in the Sarum books, 'Vide, Domine, quoniam tribulor'. As in the case of the Visitation, 'edita' should probably more accurately

1 C. M. Berti, 'De cultu Septem Dolorum S. Mariae', *Marianum* ii (1940), 81–6, reviewing evidence adduced by Wilmart, op. cit.

2 H. Delehaye, 'La Vierge aux Sept Glaives', *Analecta Bollandiana* xii (1893), 333–52.

3 Ibid. 341; for the date 1492, see a review by R. Lechat in *Anal. Boll.* xlii (1924), 220. A feast of the Compassion was permitted to the Carthusians in 1477 (for Saturday after the octave of Easter), made obligatory in 1486, and in the following year moved to the Saturday after Passion Sunday: Hourlier and Du Moustier, 'Le calendrier cartusien', 155. No influence in England is apparent.

4 *Missale Romanum 1474* ii, 281, 339, 340, 341; that beginning on p. 342 is the same as that on p. 339.

be 'approbata'; it does seem that Sixtus IV approved the mass and had the feast entered in the martyrology.[1] 'Cumque vidisset' is the mass which appears in the printed Hereford missals, 1502 and 1510, as 'Missa Nostrae Dominae Pietatis', after the common of saints: here again, as with the Visitation, following Roman forms authorized by Sixtus rather than those already in use in Sarum books. It is not certain which is the older mass or which, if either, was the one used at Cologne. (The Sarum mass is found in one manuscript English missal, but among additions which suggest that the section was copied from the printed missal.[2])

The evidence from missals, then, is that two different masses were known in England, one at least from 1497, the other at least from 1502. Neither is associated with a date, neither contains any indication of becoming a feast; neither appears in the York or Arbuthnott missals. But, to return now to the offices, that printed by Caxton between 1487 and 1491 specifies the Friday before Passion Sunday, and the office supplementary to the Aberdeen breviary stipulates the Wednesday of Holy Week. It looks as though a potential feast is contemplated in both. Rhythmical offices of the Compassion existed in as great number as those of the Visitation; Dreves collected at least ten,[3] of which two are based on 'Bonaventure's' office. This does not seem to be the entire number. Caxton's office appears to have some similarity with 'Bonaventure's', more with the Aberdeen reworking of it. The Aberdeen office adds forms for first vespers to 'Cum maria virgine', and expands what was originally a votive office into a full liturgical office of nine lessons. Yet another office is found after the litany in a (probably late) fifteenth-century Augustinian breviary from Walsingham,[4]

[1] B. Capelle in A. G. Martimort, ed., *L'Eglise en prière* (3rd edn., Paris, 1965), 780, but, as with the Visitation, no record of Sixtus's action seems to survive; the Compassion is not in Baronius's *Martyrologium Romanum* (Rome, 1586).

[2] Gonville and Caius Cbg. MS. 146 (196). A third hand has added masses of the Holy Name, Wounds, 'Recordare', Sebastian, Chrysostom, Gabriel, Antony, Mary Magdalen, David (also added earlier in a second hand), Chad, Winifred, Visitation, and (f. 752) 'de Lamentatione sive de Planctu de beate marie in morte filii'. The mass, and missal, end abruptly just after the beginning of the epistle.

[3] *AHMA* xxiv. 122–52. The rhythmical parts of the Aberdeen office are given on pp. 142–6.

[4] Keble Oxf. MS. 61, f. 188v. The office is in two parts, beginning on ff. 188 and 323.

which uses hymns not otherwise known; it too is a full liturgical office, such as would only be said on a feast, but the kalendar of the book is missing, and the rubric gives no indication of a date. Considering Walsingham's place as the centre of the Virgin's cult in England, it is not surprising that the latest Marian devotion should be included.

The Compassion seems to have come only marginally closer than the Five Wounds or the Crown of Thorns to becoming a fully accepted English feast.[1] Perhaps, lacking specific papal promulgation, or an ancient if sporadic tradition of observance, it did not have a strong enough impetus really to catch on. We shall now see how the Presentation, having slightly more of both those elements, was somewhat closer to being fully accepted in England by the close of our period.

The Presentation of the Virgin

The feast of the Presentation of the Virgin—for here we are clearly talking about what is in origin a wholly liturgical feast—is noteworthy among the observances we have discussed in several senses: its widespread promulgation in the West can be traced to a single beginning, though there was an earlier observance which survived to some degree; a good deal of precise information is available on who composed some of the liturgical forms used for the feast; and, most distinctive, there is a modern monograph on the subject.[2] The Presentation is something like the Transfiguration in its origin, something like the Visitation in certain features of its promulgation and spread; and the exiguous degree of observance it had acquired in England before the Reformation is the more instructive because of the parallels with these more widely received feasts.

The story of Mary's presentation in the Temple by her

[1] What is sometimes called an 'office' of the Compassion, 'Matris cor virgineum', is a set of eight stanzas to be worked in, after the 'office' of the Cross, following each hour-service of the Virgin in a book of hours. 'Matris cor virgineum' is printed in *AHMA* xxx. 106, and can be seen worked into the other hour-forms in *Horae Eboracenses*, passim.

[2] M. J. Kishpaugh, *The Feast of the Presentation of the Virgin Mary in the Temple* (Washington, Catholic University of America dissertation, 1941). Sr. Kishpaugh's treatment is based almost entirely on printed sources, and her discussion of the feast in England emphasizes literary evidence much more than liturgical.

parents, when she was three years old, originates in the 'infancy gospel' of the apocryphal *Book of James* ('Protevangelium'), dating probably from the second century.[1] At an early date the story was incorporated in an Eastern feast, the 'Eisodos', conjecturally connected with the dedication of the church of New St. Mary's at Jerusalem in 543, on November 21st;[2] virtually the only date to have been observed for the Presentation in either the East or the West. Whether there was a proper feast in the Eastern Church before the eighth century is subject to some disagreement, but for our purposes it is only necessary to note that the Presentation was certainly observed by then.[3]

Commemoration of such a story, filling out to a slight extent the outlines of the Virgin's life between her nativity and the Annunciation,[4] clearly fits with the tendency we have noticed in later medieval spirituality to elaborate liturgically the lives of Christ and his mother. The feast of the Presentation was introduced in the west in 1372, by the returning Crusader, Philippe de Mézières, chancellor of the Duchy of Cyprus.[5] Here Eastern origins and late medieval liturgical fashions meet conveniently and convincingly. Philippe, who seems to have been endowed with an abnormal degree of persuasiveness as well as of spiritual power,[6] convinced King Charles V of France and Pope Gregory XI to allow and encourage the feast, for which he had composed both an office and a mass. With Gregory's permission the feast was celebrated in the Franciscan church at Avignon on November 21st, 1372, and two years later Charles sent a letter to the Navarrese college at Paris, specially commending the observance.[7]

[1] Available most conveniently in M. R. James, *The Apocryphal New Testament* (Oxford, 1924), 38–49.

[2] This theory, elaborated by E. Bouvy, 'Les origines de la fête de la Présentation', *Rev. Augustinienne* i (1902), 581–94, and S. Vailhé, 'La dédicace de Sainte-Marie-la-Neuve', ibid. ii (1903), 136–40, is disputed by H. Chirat, 'Psõmia diaphora, pt. 2: Les origines de la fête du 21 Novembre', *Mélanges E. Podechard* (Lyon, 1945), 127–33.

[3] Kishpaugh, 36 ff.

[4] The espousals of Mary and Joseph was the subject of a mass which appeared in the printed Roman missal from 1558: *Missale Romanum 1474* ii. 338.

[5] Philippe himself states that he introduced the feast at Venice, but nothing more is known about this. See Kishpaugh, 95–6.

[6] The standard work on him is N. Jorga, *Philippe de Mézières (1327–1405) et la croisade au XIVe siècle* (Paris, 1896).

[7] This letter is transcribed in K. Young, *The Drama of the Medieval Church* ii (Oxford, 1933), 473–8.

But observance of the Presentation was not totally unknown in the West before the time of Philippe de Mézières. In England, especially, there was an ancient if not very widespread recognition of a feast based on the Presentation story. It can be found in pre-Conquest documents of two famous Benedictine abbeys, Christ Church (Canterbury) and Hyde (Winchester). A Christ Church benedictional of about 1030 contains a blessing, under the heading 'de Presentatione Sancte Marie', which specifically refers to the story: '. . . celebrantes hunc diem quo templum Dei sacrarium spiritus sancti in aula dei est presentatum';[1] while two Hyde kalendars, one of the early eleventh century[2] and one of about 1060,[3] include the feast under its more usual English title of 'Oblacio': 'Oblacio sancte Marie in templo domini cum esset trium annorum.' Since the feast is missing from a Hyde kalendar of *c.* 1025,[4] and from a Christ Church kalendar of 1012–23,[5] the feast must have been introduced in both places during, at most, the forty years before the Conquest. In both houses, observance, or at least recognition, continued after the Conquest as well.[6]

Pre-fifteenth-century recognition of the Presentation occurs in England for the most part in major Benedictine houses, and

[1] BM MS. Harl. 2892, f. 186; this use of the title 'Presentatio' in England before the time of Philippe de Mézières seems unique, but it is in the original MS., and is not a title supplied by the modern editor, R. M. Woolley, as one might be tempted to think (*Canterbury Benedictional* (HBS li, 1916), 116).

[2] BM MS. Cott. Tit. D. xxvii. S. J. P. van Dijk, 'The Origin of the Latin Feast of the Conception of the Blessed Virgin Mary', *Dublin Review* ccxxviii (1954), 254, dates the addition of the 'Oblacio' and the Conception to perhaps the 1050s.

[3] BM MS. Cott. Vit. E. xviii. Both this and the above kalendars are edited in Wormald, *Eng. Kals. before 1100.*

[4] Trin. Cbg. MS. 945, printed in Wormald, *Eng. Kals. before 1100.*

[5] BM MS. Arundel 155, also in Wormald, op. cit.; it has been added in a fifteenth-century hand.

[6] Christ Church kalendars in profusion: Trin. Cbg. MS. 987, pre-1170 ('Eadwine Psalter'); Bodl. MS. Add. C. 260 (early addition to pre-1170 kalendar); BN MS. lat. 770 (copy of kalendar *c.* 1220); BM MS. Cott. Tib. B. iii, pre-1220; BM MS. Eg. 2867, *c.* 1250; Bodl. MS. Auct. D. 2. 2., post-1320; Lambeth MS. 558, fourteenth–fifteenth century; BM MS. Sloane 3887, early fifteenth century; Univ. Oxf. MS. 56, fifteenth century; also Lambeth MS. 20, a martyrology, fifteenth or early sixteenth century (21 November ends 'Eodem die oblacio beate dei genetricis Mariae in templo'); and BM MS. Arundel 68, another martyrology with the entry for the 'oblacio' added to it in a different hand. There is no entry in the twelfth-century martyrology from the same house, BM MS. Roy. 7. E. vi.

The late thirteenth-century 'Hyde Breviary' (Bodl. MSS. Rawl. liturg. e. 1*, Gough liturg. 8) will be discussed later. The kalendar of a Hyde psalter of the fourteenth–fifteenth centuries (BM MS. Harl. 960) lacks November.

Edmund Bishop argued[1] that its likeliest source was Rome, because two English visits to the papal court, one royal and one archiepiscopal, preceded the earliest date for its appearance in monastic kalendars. Its presence in Italy could easily have been the result of the Greek monasteries there; there is, for instance, a tenth-century gospel-book from Cesena, near Ravenna, which includes the observance on November 21st.[2] On the other hand, the Presentation story is referred to in the section on the nativity of the Virgin in the Old English martyrology of about 900,[3] so the legend was certainly known in England before either of the two visits Bishop adduces. Henry Thurston had earlier suggested but less convincingly, that the feast came from Ireland, probably through a Coptic kalendar introduced there.[4] Thurston and Bishop agreed that the Presentation was closely linked with the Conception, and if Bishop is right in stating that both feasts disappeared in the Norman ecclesiastical settlement in England, the 'Oblacio' reappeared, at least in kalendars, within a century after the Conquest.

In fact, even disregarding the haphazardness of manuscript survival, it does look as though knowledge of a feast of the Presentation spread slightly in England in the centuries between the eleventh and fifteenth. The Hyde breviary which survives provides us with an office used for the feast there at the end of the thirteenth century,[5] and a Muchelney breviary of about the same date contains a different office.[6] The incipits of a third office are contained in the Barking Ordinal, of about a hundred years later.[7] Other liturgical documents show that the feast was at

[1] 'On the Origins of the Feast of the Conception of the Blessed Virgin Mary', *Liturgica Historica* (Oxford, 1916), 258–9.

[2] Holweck, *Cal. Liturg.* 386; H. Leclercq, 'Césène, MSS. Liturgiques de', *DACL* ii. 3310–18. The gospel prescribed is that for the Nativity of the Virgin, 'Exurgens Maria'. Another such instance of Eastern influence on the borders, so to speak, of the West probably occurs in the appearance of the Presentation in a Hungarian kalendar of *c.* 1200: M. Zalan, 'Das frühste Vorkommen des Festes Presentations BVM in Abendland', *Ephemerides Liturgicae* xli (1927), 188 ff. (summarized in Kishpaugh).

[3] *An Old English Martyrology* (EETS cxvi (1909)), 165.

[4] 'The Irish Origins of our Lady's Conception Feast', *The Month* ciii (1904), 459–60.

[5] In vol. iv of modern edition, HBS lxxviii (1939), 383–5.

[6] BM MS. Add. 43406, f. 274–7.

[7] Ed. HBS lxvi (1927), 340–1. There is, as we shall see, also a fourth office, in a Battle breviary of the late fifteenth or early sixteenth century, Trin. Cbg. MS. 1359, f. 190^{v}.

least known in a number of abbeys. At Westminster the 'Oblacio' is in the kalendar (though not the sanctorale) of the 'Westminster Missal', 1383–4,[1] but not in the kalendar of a psalter of almost 1200;[2] the distinctive title is retained in the kalendar of a later fifteenth-century book of Westminster offices, at a date when other manuscripts, if they had added it at all, would more likely have called it 'Presentatio'.[3] The Sherborne missal of the fourteenth and fifteenth centuries has the 'Oblacio' in its kalendar,[4] as do kalendars of two thirteenth-century Worcester manuscripts.[5] The Amesbury nuns in the fourteenth century observed the 'Oblacio' with twelve lessons.[6] The thirteenth-century kalendar of a Tewkesbury missal of both thirteenth and fourteenth centuries includes the feast in red in the original hand, graded at three lessons.[7] There is no office in the sanctorale, which is much shortened. As would be expected, the feast was eventually recognized at Canterbury St. Augustine's: it is found in three thirteenth- and fourteenth-century kalendars,[8] and is listed as a feast of the fourth (i.e. highest) dignity in the early fourteenth-century customary of the house.[9]

Sometimes, as we have seen, when there is no indication of observance of a feast, in a number of martyrologies a notice is either included in the original hand or added at the end of the

[1] Ed. HBS i (1891), xv.

[2] BM MS. Roy. 2. A. xii, ed. HBS xii (*Westminster Missal* iii) (1897), 1385–96, and collated in Wormald ii. 57 ff.

[3] Bodl. MS. Rawl. liturg. g. 10, printed in Wormald, loc. cit. The feast is in red, like the three principal 'nova festa'.

[4] J. W. Legg, 'Liturgical Notes on the Sherborne Missal', *Transactions St. Paul's Ecclesiological Society* iv (1896), 21.

[5] Magd. Oxf. MS. 100, a psalter, and Worcester Cathedral MS. F. 160, an antiphoner, both cited by Sr. Kishpaugh; both kalendars printed in HBS lvi (*The Leofric Collectar*) (1921), 586 ff.

[6] CUL MS. Ee. vi. 16 (Kalendar of a book of hours).

[7] CUL MS. Gg. iii. 21. The same grading is found in a Tewkesbury kalendar of the late twelfth or early thirteenth century, BM MS. Roy. 8. C. vii.

[8] St. John's Cbg. MS. 262, Canterbury Cathedral MS. E. xix, Gonville and Caius MS. 238, all printed in Wormald i. 47 ff. November is missing in the late thirteenth-century kalendar, BM MS. Cott. Jul. D. xi.

[9] Ed. HBS xxiii (*Customary of the Benedictine Monasteries of St. Augustine, Canterbury and St. Peter, Westminster*) (1902), 431, from BM MS. Cott. Faust. C. xii. Here the feast was almost certainly not as early as at Christ Church, for it is not in the missal, which the modern editor dates about 1100: *The Missal of St. Augustine's Abbey, Canterbury*, ed. M. Rule (Cambridge, 1896). 'Eodem die oblacio beatissime marie virginis' is added, but in a not much later hand, in the eleventh–twelfth-century martyrology, BM MS. Cott. Vit. C. xii.

entry for the day. We have already considered a Christ Church martyrology of that sort. A Norwich martyrology of the fifteenth century begins the entry for the day with 'Oblacio sancte marie in templo.[1] The first entry in a Cluniac martyrology from Faversham, of about 1400, is rather fuller: 'Iherosolimis elect(a?) dei Genetrix Maria virgo perpetua cum esset trium annorum oblata est domino a parentibus in templo.'[2] At this date it would have been easily possible for knowledge of Philippe de Mézière's promotion of the feast to be known, but even if this is the case it is significant that the old English title is retained. This is true of an even later instance, a secular martyrology from Bury St. Edmunds of probably the third quarter of the fifteenth century, to which there has been added 'Item oblacio sancte marie virgine in templo cum esset trium annorum'.[3] But the fifteenth-century Syon martyrology[4] ends the entry for November 21st 'Item presentacio sancte marie in templo', in what appears to be the original hand (the first three words seem to have been erased and written over again).

The fact that there are a certain number of English manuscript mentions of the 'Presentatio' under that name proves that the same feast was known by both names in England (though no case has been encountered of a formula like 'Oblacio sive Presentatio'.) The manuscript York missal from Nottinghamshire has, added to the kalendar in faint black ink, 'Presentacio sancte Marie virginis'.[5] 'Presentacio' is in red ink in a Sarum-type kalendar of the early fifteenth century,[6] and in a book of hours of the same century from the north-east of England, the kalendar of which has a saint for each day.[7] But 'Oblacio' as a title was never superseded. It even appears in at least two Benedictine manuscripts of the beginning of the sixteenth century or thereabouts, the Battle breviary we have already noticed,[8] and the kalendar of a Shaftesbury book of hours.[9]

[1] BM MS. Cott. Jul. B. vii.

[2] Bodl. MS. Jones 9. Faversham was constitutionally Benedictine, but was colonized from Bermondsey and probably followed Cluniac liturgical customs.

[3] Bodl. MS. Rawl. liturg. e. 42.

[4] BM MS. Add. 22285. The feast had not been in the kalendar of a Syon book of hours of the second quarter of the fifteenth century, Bodl. MS. Rawl. C. 781.

[5] Univ. Oxf. MS. 78B.

[6] Bodl. MS. Ashmole 5.

[7] Bodl. MS. Gough liturg. 3.

[8] Trin. Cbg. MS. 1359, ff. 190v–192.

[9] Fitzwilliam Mus. Cbg. MS. 2-1957.

Awareness of the feast outside Benedictine houses was not confined to martyrological notices.[1] A kalendar of St. Elizabeth's college, Winchester, of perhaps the mid-fifteenth century, probably shows Hyde influence when it includes (apparently on November 22nd), 'Oblacio sancte marie virginis . . . ix le(ctiones)'.[2] Again, the early fifteenth-century Carmelite breviary, probably from Cambridge, has 'Oblacio B.V.M. totum duplex' added to the kalendar in the same hand which has added the Visitation.[3] The kalendar of a fourteenth/fifteenth-century Augustinian collectar from Llanthony (Glos.) has the 'Oblacio' in red in the original hand, while the principal 'nova festa' have been added.[4] Another Augustinian kalendar, probably from Tonbridge, of after 1457—Osmund is in the original hand, with grading—has the 'Oblacio' added to it, along with the Transfiguration and Holy Name, in a hand much the same as the original.[5]

The most noteworthy non-Benedictine observance of the 'Oblacio' occurs in the diocese of Exeter. When John de Grandisson, Bishop of Exeter, founded the collegiate church of Ottery St. Mary in 1339 he decreed specially that three feasts should be observed: St. Gabriel, St. Anne, and 'Eodem modo fiat in crastino sancti Edmundi regis et martyris [i.e. Novemver 21st] missa de oblacione beate marie Virginis'.[6] In the

[1] In one instance it is indicated only pictorially. In a fragment of an elaborately illuminated fifteenth-century gospel lectionary which belonged to Salisbury Cathedral (BM MS. Harl. 7026), at the vigil of the Assumption (f. 14) there is a miniature of Anna and Joachim with the young Mary about to ascend seven steps to an altar.

[2] Bodl. MS. Lat. misc. e. 22.

[3] Univ. Oxf. MS. 9. The Carmelites had accepted the feast as early as 1393, and it was promoted to 'totum duplex' in 1420: Kallenberg, 45, 48. If the ascription of this MS. is correct, it is an interesting example of the old English name for the feast being retained for the observance directly inspired by Philippe de Mézières.

[4] Corpus Christi Oxf. MS. 192.

[5] Stockholm Roy. Lib. MS. A. 182. I owe knowledge of this manuscript and of the particulars about it to the kindness of Mr. Christopher Hohler.

[6] G. Oliver, *Monasticon Dioecesis Exon.* (Exeter, 1846), 269, no. 17. Sr. Kishpaugh, 88, missed the significance of the abbreviated note in the *Westminster Missal* iii. 1446, that the 'Oblacio' was 'kept at Sherb. & Aug. . . . also St. Mary Otterie'. A boss in the centre of the choir at Ottery depicts the Presentation: J. N. Dalton, *The Collegiate Church of Ottery St. Mary* (Cambridge, 1917), 145. Grandisson bought the plot of land for Ottery St. Mary from the chapter of Rouen (G. Oliver, *Lives of the Bishops of Exeter* (Exeter, 1861), 80). A breviary of St. Amand, Rouen, of the late thirteenth century (BN MS. lat. 1027; Leroquais, *Brevs.* iii. 1) contains the 'Oblacio' with an office of twelve lessons, in the original hand. Leroquais remarks on the rarity of this.

ordinal which he had composed for Exeter cathedral two years earlier, observance of the 'Oblacio' is ordered for the Lady Chapel in similar terms, and three of the mass forms are specified: the epistle is to be 'Ab inicio' or 'Egreditur virga', the alleluia 'Virga iesse', and the gospel 'Dixit Maria, Magnificat' (Luke 1: 46 ff.?).[1] The first of the epistles and the alleluia verse have, as we shall see, the same incipits as those of the Barking mass of about sixty years later.

We are now in a position to face the obvious question: how much was the incipient acceptance of the Presentation as a new feast in England by the close of the fifteenth century due to the indigenous, though not widespread, English tradition and how much to the continental influence resulting from the energies of Philippe de Mézières? The large 'totum' editions of the Sarum breviary of 1496 Rouen, 1516 Paris, and 1531 Paris include an office of the Presentation,[2] followed by the mass of the feast. All three have the office in the same place,[3] among the special 'commemorations' following the 'Servitium' of the Virgin: Commemoration of Thomas of Canterbury, Translation and Commemoration of Chad, 'in festo Yconiae Domini Salvatoris', and Presentation. Only the 1498 (London) Sarum Missal prints a mass of the Presentation[4] (which is identical to that in the very similar Arbuthnott missal of 1491, after the votive masses and along with those of David and Chad). The printed Sarum hours, from the early edition of 1495, include the Presentation in the kalendars, in all editions until those of 1539 to 1549, and reappearing in the editions of 1551 to 1560. It is also in the kalendars of three Sarum processionals, 1506, 1530, and 1555, but not in those of the 1490(?) or 1504 editions. What factors best account for this sporadic but not negligible recognition?

[1] *Ordinale Exon.* ii (HBS xxxviii, 1909), 474–5. Grandisson may have had a special devotion to this feast, for it is probable that he consecrated his new cathedral on 21 November 1367 (*DNB* viii. 372). But the feast does not appear in the kalendar or sanctorale of the Ordinal, and its observance seems to have been confined to the Lady Chapel.

[2] It is likely that the 1497 Rouen edition was going to contain the office, but only the winter part survives. At the end of the table of psalms there follows a list of more or less new feasts, none of which is included in the kalendar: Presentation, St. Mary of the Snows, St. Osmund, 'Festum Salvatoris', Name of Jesus, St. Chad.

[3] *Sarum Breviary* ii. 329. The woodcut in the 1516 and 1531 breviaries (not included in the modern edition) is of the Circumcision.

[4] *Sarum Missal*, 915*.

The office printed in the Sarum breviaries is Philippe's rhythmical composition, beginning 'Fons hortorum'. This, like two other offices he composed, is an acrostic exercise: in this case, the initial letters of (at first vespers) the five antiphons to the psalms, the versicle and response following, the five stanzas of the vespers hymn, and the antiphon to the Magnificat, and of (at matins) the invitatory, the five stanzas of that hymn and the antiphons and responds to the seven lessons, are meant to spell out 'Frater Rostagnus (one of Philippe's pen-names) virginem toto corde magnificat'.[1] A similar feat is performed in the sequence 'Altissime providente', where the first lines of the successive stanzas spell out 'Ave Maria benedico te Amen'. The Sarum office runs substantially like that in Philippe's autograph.[2] Between the office and the mass there comes the 'Gesta de presentatione beatae Mariae': the first six chapters of the Gospel of Pseudo-Matthew,[3] the Latin 'Infancy gospel' which draws heavily on the *Protevangelium* but with distinctive touches by which its influence can be traced, notably the fifteen steps of the Temple which Mary ascends. The Sarum text, however, lacks the rubric at the end of the last section of the 'Gesta' stating that it was to be read at the conclusion of the mystery play which preceded the mass: the 'representatio figurata' which Philippe records having earlier produced at Venice.[4] This omission means that the 'Gesta' stands in the Sarum breviary totally without explanation or rationale, and it may be that the entire text was taken from another service book, of a use in which the play was still performed and the 'Gesta' read.

The rubric which begins the Sarum office mentions four

[1] Text in *AHMA* lii. 44. This does not in fact work in the Sarum text, because the response and versicle after the antiphons at first vespers are omitted, and the third stanza of the hymn at vespers has been altered, as in many of the MSS. of this office, probably to guard against any possible doubt of the Immaculate Conception being raised by the original line: 'Tollens a matre fomitis / Labem dum alvo clauditur': see Blume's note in *AHMA*, ut sup. Evidently the acrostic character of the office was not regarded as an inviolable feature, if indeed it was always recognized.

[2] BN MS. lat. 17330, which has not been edited yet, though Sr. Kishpaugh has an edition in preparation. She has kindly supplied me with a comparison between Philippe's original text and that of the Sarum Breviary.

[3] Ed. C. Tischendorf, *Evangelica Apocrypha* (2nd edn., Leipzig, 1876), 54–64.

[4] Kishpaugh, 98–9; the play has been edited by K. Young, *Drama Med. Ch.* ii. 227–45; cf. his article, 'Philippe de Mézières's Dramatic Office for the Presentation of the Virgin', *Publications of the Modern Language Association* xxvi (1911), 181–234.

historical facts, all of them (for a change) apparently true, but none concerned with Philippe de Mézières. The rubric reads that the king of France caused the feast to be celebrated in his presence, and sent the office to the great churches of his kingdom, and to the emperor, who promised that he would have it celebrated and publicized. The king also sent the office to the 'old queen of Hungary' ('reginae antiquae Hungariae': the queen-mother Elizabeth) who commanded its celebration there. The king of France referred to is clearly Charles V, as we have seen; he died in 1380, and Elizabeth of Hungary in 1387, while of the Holy Roman Emperors Charles IV died in 1378 and Wenceslaus IV in 1419. What are commemorated in this rubric, then, are events of the fifteen years after the first observance of the Presentation at Avignon; yet the principal promoter of the feast is not mentioned, through either self-effacement or neglect.

The office in the Aberdeen breviary, included in its proper place in the sanctorale and listed as a minor double in the kalendar, is also substantially Philippe's office, with the lessons shortened and with some changes. The most notable of the latter are to be found in the collect, which is totally different, and in the capitula. The capitulum at first vespers is S. of S. 2 : 4–5 instead of Ecclus. 24 : 23, and that at second vespers is Ecclus. 24 : 30–1. The comparatively brief lessons in the first two nocturns can be found in Sarum lessons i and iii, respectively, while those for the third nocturn are taken from Bede's commentary on Matthew 1, which provides the gospel for both the Nativity and Presentation of the Virgin. Philippe's hymns for first vespers, 'O Dei sapientia', and for second vespers, 'Aeterni patris ordine', are combined (the acrostic scheme is apparently of no concern), and the whole hymn repeated at both vespers.

But the most interesting thing about the Aberdeen office is that the responsory after lesson ix is not the corresponding number in the Sarum office—the first eight responsories have been identical in both—but is one of the three rhythmical responsories which is printed after responsory ix of matins in the Sarum office (which then concludes with the missing response and versicle from first vespers). This would lead one to suspect that there might have been a twelve-lesson version of the office, though all of the large number of manuscripts Blume collated contain only nine responsories. But it is certainly possible that the influence of a monastic office (since the monastic rite had twelve lessons at matins of important feasts) may have been at work here.

There were, indeed, several English monastic offices of twelve lessons for this feast: we have briefly noticed those of Hyde, Muchelney, Barking, and (very late) Battle. Of the Hyde and Barking offices it is chiefly the incipits which survive.[1] But we can tell that the office which Philippe de Mézières composed is independent of all these offices (except, as we shall shortly notice, that they all share the same collect). The Hyde office is taken largely from that of the Nativity of the Virgin, with the notable exceptions of the collect, the lessons, and the unbiblical capitulum at none, 'Beata dei genetrix maria hodierna die deo oblata quasi sydus eximium inter fluctus seculi labentis gracia privilegii specialis effulsit.' The lessons of the first two nocturns are taken from what appears to be a homily proper to the story, while the last four are (though this is not specified) presumably from a commentary on one of the two alternative gospels whose incipits are given: 'Loquente ihesu ad turbas', or 'Exurgens maria'. Neither of these two gospels is encountered elsewhere for the feast. The collect (also specified in the Barking office for lauds, terce, and second vespers) is the most noteworthy feature: it is a slightly expanded version of the same prayer which, according to John of Würzburg (fl. 1160–70) was used in the church of the Holy Sepulchre in Jerusalem.[2] He specifies that the feast is observed on November 21st; and the verb he uses is 'oblata', though the collect uses 'presentari': 'In hoc ipso templo Domini Christi XI. Kalend. Decembris dicitur beata virgo Maria jam, trium annorum parvula, oblata fuisse a Deo, ut hi versiculi docent ibidem inscripti: "Virginibus septem Virgo comitata puellis, / Servitura Deo fuit his oblata triennis."'[3] The same prayer is also used in Philippe's office (his mass collect is different). The Hyde collect, then, had been in existence for over a century by the time that breviary was compiled; and the prayer is not of English origin unless it travelled to the Holy Land from there, which is improbable though not impossible.

[1] Sr. Kishpaugh has expanded the incipits of the Hyde office and prints the reconstituted office on pp. 83–7 of her monograph. The Muchelney office seems to be very like the Hyde; it is of roughly the same date.

[2] *PL* clv. 1090.

[3] Ibid. 1062.

The extent of the improbability is difficult to judge. No liturgical forms survive for an English observance previous to the Hyde office, except the episcopal benediction from the 'Canterbury Benedictional' which we have already noticed. We have seen that the observance of the 'Oblacio' seems to have been confined to Winchester and Canterbury before the Conquest. Now, it is well known that a considerable number of Englishmen went to Constantinople after the Conquest, mostly to serve in the Varangian Guard. It is likely that they carried Latin service books with them, for we know that a small 'English' church, dedicated to SS. Nicholas and Augustine, was built in Constantinople; and we know furthermore that the man who built it was educated at St. Augustine's, Canterbury.[1] It is not impossible that he (for example; there are doubtless others of whom we do not know) might have brought with him forms for the 'Oblacio' in use at Christ Church. What this hypothetical reconstruction leaves out is how the English collect for the 'Oblacio', assuming that it got to Constantinople, would have passed from there to Jerusalem by the 1160s. This, however, especially considering that the (Crusaders') Latin patriarchs of Jerusalem lived in Constantinople, is hardly insuperable.

If this chain of conjecture should be correct (it is unlikely that it could ever be proved or disproved) we should be faced with a rather extraordinary circular movement. The feast, which was Eastern in origin, was known among the Greek-speaking monasteries in Italy by the tenth century; from there it passed to a limited observance in England probably around the middle of the eleventh century. Whether the Latin prayers used for the feast (probably only prayers were needed, since other forms could be taken from those for the Nativity of the Virgin, as happened in the early observance of the Conception) were composed in England or elsewhere is not known. In any case, English refugees could have taken the forms with them to Constantinople, whence they could have passed into use at Jerusalem by the mid-twelfth century. Indeed, they were possibly in general use among Latin-speaking Christians of the

[1] C. H. Haskins, 'A Canterbury Monk at Constantinople', *English Historical Review* xxv (1910), 294, n. 5; *AA. SS. Mai* vi (1686), 410. The setting is elaborated in A. A. Vasiliev, 'The Opening Stages of the Anglo-Saxon Immigration to Byzantium in the Eleventh Century', *Annales de l'Institut Kondakov* ix (1937), 60–1. According to Janin, 591, the site is unknown.

Levant. Philippe de Mézières, becoming devoted to an observance not generally recognized in the West, and not having a proper mass and office, may have incorporated what did exist, notably the collect, in his own office. (The mass-collect is different.) When these were printed in late Sarum breviaries, consequently, the collect of the office would have been the same as that which had been in use, though sporadically, since at least the revival of the feast in twelfth-century England.

The immediate cause of the Presentation's becoming even an incipient new feast in England at the end of our period was probably neither Philippe's promotion nor the vestiges of the old observance, but the Marian devotion of Sixtus IV. He took up the cause of the Presentation, as he did also of the Visitation and the Compassion, and promulgated it anew in 1472[1]—though once again, as in the case of the other feasts, it is difficult to tell what the exact extent of his promulgation was. The 1505 printed Roman missal contains a mass 'In festo presentationis virginis Marie quod festum institutum a Sixto papa quarto':[2] but the mass which follows is Philippe's, including the sequence. The mass is also in the 1508 Roman missal, but subsequent editions have the mass of the Nativity of the Virgin, 'Mutato nomine nativitatis in nomen presentationis', or a new mass (in editions after 1543 only). But none of these forms had, as far as we know, much currency in England.[3]

[1] Bäumer ii. 110, and references there.

[2] *Missale Romanum 1474* ii. 251. The 1505 Roman breviary is more specific: the rubric preceding Philippe's office tells how, after the feast spread from France, in 'anglia hispania atque in aliis partibus mundi: nunc novit et sanctissimus papa sixtus quartus ipsum publicavit: ut per totum mundi fieri debeat'.

[3] An exception is the English Premonstratensians, who established the feast, with a grading of nine lessons, at their Provincial Chapter at Lincoln in 1495; the forms were to be those for the Nativity of the Virgin, with 'Presentation' substituted in the appropriate places: *Collectanea Anglo-Premonstratensia* i. 175. The late Battle office (Benedictine) of the 'Oblacio' seems very much like that for the Virgin's Nativity, but it is more likely that it is a remnant of the old English monastic observance than a symptom of a new devotion.

VI

THE FEAST OF THE 'ICONIA DOMINI SALVATORIS'

IN the last chapter we noticed that the office of the Presentation was preceded in the printed Sarum breviaries which contained it (1496, 1516, 1531) by an office entitled 'In festo Yconiae Domini Salvatoris'. These two follow the Commemorations of St. Thomas Becket and St. Chad, and the Translation of the latter, between the psalter and the common of saints. The office is also, as we shall see, contained in the 1497 Rouen edition, under a different title. The 'Iconia Domini Salvatoris' was an incipient feast, like those considered in the last chapter, but of such a puzzling nature, and eventually of such interest, that it deserves a chapter to itself.

The story which the nine lessons tell[1] is of an image of Christ in Beirut which was subjected to a re-enactment of the Passion. Briefly, a Christian who lives next to a synagogue puts this image in his bedroom, and forgets it when he leaves his lodgings and is succeeded in them by a Jew. One of the latter's fellow Jews, discovering the image which the tenant had not noticed, denounces him to the chief priests, who proceed to inflict on the image the same indignities to which their forefathers had subjected Christ. When the side of the depicted Lord is pierced with a spear, blood and water pour forth, which heal the paralyzed, possessed, and blind to whom it is applied. This causes the mass conversion of the city's Jews, who apply *en bloc* to the bishop for baptism. All the synagogues are reconsecrated as Christian churches.

As far as is known, the tale was first introduced at the Second Council of Nicaea in 787, in the midst of the iconoclastic controversy.[2] It was offered, in the form of a sermon attributed (for effect) to Athanasius, by Peter, Bishop of Nicomedia. At the conclusion of the sermon, which is considerably longer than the

[1] *Sarum Breviary* ii. 323 ff.

[2] Mansi xiii. 23–32 and 580–5.

aggregate of the breviary lessons, Bishop Constantine of Constantia in Cyprus declared that the account had made the whole council to recognize, with prickings of conscience and tears, that images can be highly effectual.

To straighten out all the versions and traditions of this story is beyond the scope of this book, but enough details are available to establish the facts we need. It seems undeniable that the story was used at the Second Nicene Council, and it may have its origins in either an historical event of some sort in the two or three decades preceding 787, or in the propaganda war about images which was going on for some time before the Council. Three dates help to establish these suggestions: John of Damascus, who died about 749, does not mention the story—as Syrian pride would most likely have compelled him to do had he known it[1]—in his writings on images; Theodore of Studios, writing before 826, uses the story twice;[2] and the twelfth-century chronicler Sigebert dates the event at 765,[3] with what may be totally fanciful precision but giving a date which falls between the *termini* of 749 and 826. In 873 Anastasius Bibliothecarius translated the acta of the Council into Latin;[4] so that whether there was an earlier Latin version or not, and wherever it was composed,[5] by the late ninth century the story is known at Rome, as it were 'officially'.

Anastasius's version, like the two Greek texts of the pseudo-Athanasian sermon which Migne (following the Montfaucon edition of Athanasius) prints,[6] lacks two elements which are found in other redactions: an elaborate chain of ownership for the image, stretching from Nicodemus to Gamaliel to James to Simeon to Zaccheus to King Agrippa, and finally to Beirut;[7] and the proclamation of the establishment of the feast, to be observed on November 9th, in celebration of the miracle. The first addition can be found in the first of the two Latin texts (as

[1] This was pointed out by Baronius, *Annales* ix (Lucca, 1743), 209.

[2] *Antirrheticus* II: *PG* xcix. 365; *Epist.* II: ibid. 1605.

[3] *PL* clx. 145.

[4] *PL* cxxix. 283 ff.

[5] This question, and other matters concerning the tradition of the story and its early liturgical celebration in continental Europe, will, it is hoped, be dealt with in a subsequent study.

[6] *PG* xxviii. 796 ff.

[7] E. von Dobschütz, *Christusbilder* (*Texte und Untersuchungen* xviii, 1899), 280**, n. 2. Von Dobschütz's brief but immensely learned discussion takes place from the oblique angle of Nicodemus' role in the story.

opposed to the translations parallel to the Greek) which Migne prints among the 'Spuria' of Athanasius;[1] the second, the promulgation of the feast, is in both Latin texts there, though in slightly different forms. The provenance of the image was apparently introduced to extend the artistic activities which were assigned to Nicodemus by later legend. It is of no further importance to us, since it does not appear in the late medieval liturgical versions we are concerned with—nor, in fact, does the second addition, establishing the feast.

But this second addition is of more importance for the liturgical aspect of the story. If it is remembered that the context is a sermon supposedly written by Athanasius, read by a Bishop of Nicomedia, at a council in Nicaea, it will be seen what an odd note the conclusion of the shorter Latin version in Migne's edition sounds: 'Decrevit sancta Romana et Antiochensia [the province which included Beirut] Ecclesia diem .V. iduum Novembrium solemnem agi, in quo haec facta sunt ad laudem Domini nostri Jesu Christi, qui vivit . . .' The longer Latin version contains no reference to specific churches, but declares that the feast should be celebrated with no less reverence than Christmas and Easter.

The choice of the ninth of November can scarcely be pure coincidence with the date observed as the dedication of the Lateran basilica—that is, of the old basilica, St. Saviour's, destroyed by earthquake in 896 and replaced by the church of the present dedication to St. John Baptist. It is difficult to say whether the date assigned for the commemoration of the Beirut miracle preceded that assigned for the (old) Lateran dedication, or whether the dedication date controlled the choice of a date for the Iconia story.[2] Certainly by the twelfth century the two elements in the liturgical observance of November 9th had become thoroughly intertwined, as continental service books with entries like 'salvatoris mundi' in the kalendar and 'passio imaginis' in the sanctorale indicate.[1] The influence of the Lateran dedication would of course be most strongly felt in central Italy, but in the south of France and in eastern and

[1] *PG* xxviii. 813 ff.

[2] In the Eastern churches the story is read on Orthodoxy Sunday (first Sunday in Lent) and the November observance is apparently purely Western.

[3] Ebner, 40: twelfth-century enlarged sacramentary from Camaldoli.

northern Spain observance of what is unambiguously the 'passio imaginis' story can be seen from the eleventh century, sometimes on November 9th and sometimes (as 'Salvatoris') on November 25th.[1]

Celebration of the 'Iconia' feast did not spread throughout Europe, and into England, as extensively as did the Transfiguration, but the story was widely known, and is encountered in a number of oblique ways, some of which shed light on the (barely) incipient observance in England about 1500. John of Würzburg's 'description' of Beirut (*c.* 1160) includes a variant version of our story:

In Beryto quaedam Salvatoris nostri imago, haud multum post passionem ejus, a quibusdam Judaeis sub Crucifixi effigie ignominiose et ridiculose posita sanguinem sudavit et aquam: quae causa fuit ut Sidoniorum multi, in verum Jesum crucifixum credentes, sacrum baptismi lavacrum susceperint. Quicunque etiam ex stilla dictae imaginis peruncti fuerunt, sani fiebant, a quacunque detinebantur infirmitate;[2]

though he does not cite any service forms for a feast connected with this story. Further from the supposed site of the occurrence, the emphasis of the story—and its analogues, of which there are many—is less on the conversion of the Jews than on the prized relics which vials of the miraculous blood became. Such vials were dispersed from Constantinople to Venice[3] and Paris (and probably to Namur and St. Denis as well),[4] but possession of these relics did not, as far as we know, lead to a liturgical commemoration of the story. In Norway, however, there may have been a feast on November 9th:[5] for, as the 1519 *Breviarium Nidrosiense* tells us, when the archbishop of Trondheim returned from the Second Council of Lyons (1274) with a crystal copy of

[1] The Spanish instances seem earlier than any French ones Leroquais has noted —'Passio imaginis' Nov. 9th: Ripoll Sacramentary, *c.* 1050, ed. A. Olivar, *Mon. Hisp. Sacra.* serie liturg. vii (1964) and San Millan kalendar *c.* 1090, ed. J. Janini, *Hisp. Sacra.* xv (1962), 177–95; 'Salvatoris' Nov. 25th: kalendars (Silos and elsewhere) of 1039, 1052, 1055, and 1067, collated J. Vives, *Anal. Sacra Tarracon.* xiv (1944), 31–58.

[2] *PL* clv. 1069.

[3] De Riant, *Exuviae* ii. 150–1, 267–8. See 'Berytus' and 'Sanguis (S.) ex imagine Berytensi effusus' in index to vol. ii for numerous references. No feast relating to the blood was observed at Venice on November 9th; rather there were commemorations in March and on the vigil of the Ascension (pp. 292, 302).

[4] Ibid. 134, 68, 265.

[5] Ibid. 4; G. Storm, *Monumenta Historica Norvegiae* (Kristiana, 1880), 162.

the Crown of Thorns for Bergen Cathedral, its enshrinement could not take place on November 9th because it was found 'quod ipso die habetur memoria illius preclari miraculi, quod non longe ab Antiocha apud civitatem Berittum contigit, de iconia, in qua Dominice passionis opprobria per Iudeos renovata fuit, ut ex cronicis haberi potest, anno Domini septingentisimo quinquagesimo'. The version given here brings up once again the confusion with the dedication of the Lateran:

Et quia miraculum istud in multis ecclesiis, etiam Rome, in ecclesia Sancti Salvatoris recolitur [the miracle is then related] . . . Rome [*sic*?] in ecclesia Sancti Salvatoris a Iudeis conversis ad fidem per istud miraculum, cum isto sanguine, tradito, hodierna die conservatur, & solenne festum in memoriam Dominice passionis, ac in huius miraculi venerationem, quinto idus Novembri agitur.

Here, then, it is clearly stated that the connection between November 9th and the Lateran basilica is the commemoration of the Beirut miracle. However, it should be remembered that the story is here included in the lessons for the feast of the Crown of Thorns, which superseded the earlier commemoration after all; there is no longer (1519) a feast of the image, so that the witness is, in a sense, second-hand.[1] In both the ascription to the year 750 and the suggestion that the blood was placed in St. Saviour's at Rome, the Norwegian breviary follows the *Legenda Aurea*, in the chapter on the Exaltation of the Cross.[2] The chapter ends: 'Unde et Romae consecrata ecclesia est in honore salvatoris, ubi ampulla cum illo sanguine reservatur et solemne festum agitur.' Alternative dates, November 27th or 9th, are given—there is no indication of why.

We have now seen how the feast of the 'Iconia Domini' on November 9th combines elements of the remembrance of a miracle, the dedication of a great church, the translation of Prized relics, devotion to the Instruments of the Passion (cf. the Paris hymn for the feast of relics on September 30th: 'Nos ad laudes praeclara / Corona monet . . . Veneremus sanguinem / Et sacram harundinem / Salvatoris'),[3] and, in the *Legenda*

[1] There is, however, a nice touch of at least 'corroborative verisimilitude': the enshrinement of the imitation Crown of Thorns was to have taken place on November 4th, but it had to be postponed because of bad weather and the Archbishop's consequent delay in reaching Bergen.

[2] Cap. cxxxvii, pp. 608–9.

[3] De Riant, *Exuviae* ii. 48.

Aurea, some connection with the much older feasts of the Cross. (We shall notice that the mass of the 'Iconia' largely derives from the masses of the Cross.) There seems, perhaps, to be one additional element, which is only vaguely discernible: a confusion with the Transfiguration, as being pre-eminently a feast of the Saviour. This will be discussed presently.

Evidence of awareness of this observance in England before the first Sarum breviary to contain the office, in 1496, is extremely scanty. Martyrological additions provide the most numerous examples. The late twelfth-century martyrology which has been ascribed to the Augustinians of St. Osyth's[1] has, added to the margin in a slightly (?) later hand, 'In biretto civitate miracula domini salvatoris'. The kalendar of this manuscript contains the incipits for each feast which had a mass from the common of saints, and, as we saw, the incipits for the mass of the Transfiguration have been added, but nothing similar has been done for the 'Iconia' feast. Three other martyrologies use exactly the same phrase for their notice of the occurrence, which is in each case in the original hand in the entry for November 9th: that which Robert Elyot, fellow of Eton, bought in 1489;[2] that which was written before 1472 and belonged to a parish church of Bury St. Edmunds (St. Mary's?);[3] and, most interesting, that which belonged to the Cluniac house of St. Saviour's Bermondsey, written late in the first half of the fifteenth century.[4] The latter book has added to it at August 6th: 'Eodem die sanctus [*sic*] salvatoris: sanctus [*sic*] crucis de bermondseye ex london [?]'; then, in a third hand, 'Et Transfiguracio Domini nostri jesu Christi'.

There was a famous image, probably a crucifix, at Bermondsey which according to legend was washed ashore there in 1117.[5] The house was founded in 1082 (the first monks arrived in 1089), as a daughter house of La Charité-sur-Loire. The question is what possible connections there are between the 'Rood of Bermondsey', the dedication of the house, and these

1 Bodl. MS. Laud misc. 240. It was argued in the chapter on the Transfiguration that this ascription is probably correct.

2 Bodl. MS. Bodl. 731.

3 Bodl. MS. Rawl. liturg. e. 42.

4 Bodl. MS. Rawl. A. 371 (not included in Ker).

5 *VCH Surrey* ii. 64–77; R. Graham, 'The Priory of La Charité-sur-Loire and the Monastery of Bermondsey', *Journal of the British Archaeological Association*, N.S. xxxii (1926), 157–91, esp. pp. 175–6.

two entries in its martyrology. It appears that a number of monastic houses founded in the tenth and eleventh centuries were dedicated to St. Saviour,[1] and it is possible that this may be due to the Beirut story, or the dedication of the Lateran, or the confusion between them. Now, 'the Saviour' is iconographically most often represented by the image of Christ blessing, as in Bermondsey seals of the thirteenth, fourteenth, and fifteenth centuries.[2] But on the reverse of these seals the Transfiguration is depicted. Rose Graham pointed out that the Transfiguration is rarely seen on a seal, and compared a similar picture on the thirteenth-century seal of Faversham Abbey, which was colonized from Bermondsey in 1148, and also dedicated to St. Saviour;[3] her suggestion was that both were perhaps influenced by the twelfth-century tympanum at La Charité.[4] Whether this is true or not, what is striking is the relation between the depiction of the Transfiguration and the dedication to St. Saviour, which is also conveyed by the Bermondsey martyrology entry. Equally striking is that the tradition indicated by the Bermondsey book does not connect the Beirut miracle with the house's dedication to the Saviour. If we compare with this a puzzling entry for August *7th* in the martyrology of another monastery dedicated to St. Saviour, that near Rieti in Italy (San Salvator Maggiore)[5]—'Eodem die huius basilice domini Salvatoris' (in the original hand; the Transfiguration is entered on August 6th)—it will be seen that there does appear to be some kind of play on the word 'Salvator' as applicable to both an August and a November feast in these two houses of that dedication at Rieti and Bermondsey.[6]

The only English kalendars in which any mention of the 'Iconia' feast has been found are from two nunneries, both in

[1] See L. H. Cottineau, *Répertoire topo-bibliographique des abbayes et prieurés* (Mâcon, 1935–), 2874–5, 2879–81.

[2] Described in *VCH* ut sup. 77.

[3] The early fifteenth-century Faversham martyrology, Bodl. MS. Jones 9, contains an entry for the Transfiguration but nothing relevant for November 9th.

[4] Op. cit. 184.

[5] Bodl. MS. Lat. liturg. d. 6. The entry for November 9th begins 'Festivitas Domini Salvatoris'.

[6] According to Grotefend (*Zeitrechnung* II. ii. 89) the feast of August 6th in the diocese of Rouen was called 'Salvatoris festum'. As we saw, the altar at St. Albans which was perhaps dedicated to the Transfiguration and the Visitation is also called in one account 'In honore Sancti Salvatoris et Transfigurationis', *Amundesham Annales* i. 445.

Wiltshire, in which the Transfiguration was also early recognized. At Amesbury, which was a cell of Fontrevault from 1177 to 1403, a psalter originally of about 1220[1] has had added 'Salvatoris festum' to St. Theodore on November 9th; but van Dijk suggests that the kalendar was adapted for Franciscan nuns in a fourteenth-century hand,[2] so this piece of evidence is not conclusive. However, an Amesbury kalendar of the fourteenth century[3] corroborates notice of the feast there, for it reads at November 9th 'Perferacio sancte crucis [?] xii lectiones', followed by Theodore; the word after 'sancte' is indistinct, and 'perf*e*racio' is a misspelling, but the piercing of the image (crucifix?) seems quite clearly what is meant. It is likely that the feast was also known at Wilton. The early-fourteenth-century processional of which all that now remains is a transcript at Solesmes had the proper of saints intercalated with the temporale, and between November 6th and 11th (f. 149[v]) there were commemorated the 'miracles of the Holy Cross'.[4] But the 'Wilton Psalter' of the thirteenth century[5] does not mention the feast. The feast of the 'Iconia' can be said to have been virtually unknown in English manuscript books.

When the office for the 'Iconia Domini' appeared in the 1496 Sarum breviary, therefore, its presence must have seemed a very puzzling innovation. There was no introductory rubric, as in the case of the office of the Presentation, nor was there any indication of when the feast was to be observed. There was, further, no mass in any Sarum missal to correspond to the breviary office. The office is almost certainly complementary to the mass which appeared in the Roman missal printed at Venice in 1505,[6] and in subsequent editions of 1508, 1509, 1543,

[1] Bodl. MS. Liturg. 407.

[2] It is possible that if more Franciscan MS. evidence survived there would be more notices of this feast, or at least of the Dedication of the Lateran. A late thirteenth-century Franciscan kalendar from Richmond, Yorkshire (Bodl. MS. Rawl. liturg. e. 1) has among many fifteenth-century additions, 'Dedicacio basilice Salvatoris' after Theodore at November 9th.

[3] CUL MS. Ee. vi. 16.

[4] Benoit-Castelli, 'Un Processional Anglais . . . , *Eph. Liturg.* lxxv (1961), 281–326.

[5] Royal College of Physicians MS. 409; kalendar printed in Millar, 'Les manuscrits . . . , *Bull. de la Soc. Fr. de Reprods. de MSS. à peintures* (4th year, 1914–20), 129–34.

[6] *Missale Romanum 1474* ii. 329. However, the Roman breviary of 1505 has in the kalendar both S. Salvator at May 23rd (this will be discussed later) and the

1558, and 1560, all printed at Venice. The mass 'In solemnitate Iconie domini nostri salvatoris' is set before that of the Five Wounds. It is composed from the masses of the Cross—Invention, Exaltation, and votive—and from the Holy Week liturgy. The introit begins with the Good Friday 'trisagion', and its Pauline 'psalm-verse', 'Nos autem gloriari', like the verses of the gradual and like the offertory, are taken from these two sources. So is the communio ('Redemptor mundi'), but it is, curiously, identical with that in the masses of the Cross in the Westminster missal rather than in the Sarum or Roman uses. The gospel is Sarum and Roman for the Exaltation and the epistle that for the Sarum votive of the Trinity. Just the three prayers are proper only to this mass. Connections between the (Sarum) office and the (Roman) mass are of the usual type. They share the same collect, and the capitula add up to form the verses which comprise the epistle (Rom. 11 : 33–6). Moreover, the versicle and response after the capitulum at sext and the antiphon to the Magnificat at second vespers are close echoes of the gradual (particularly the repetition of the somewhat unexpected phrase 'Qui salvasti Petrum in mari'). But the mass never appeared in an English book.

This was not the situation in Scotland, in two important respects. First, the Aberdeen Breviary, which is for the most part a copy of the Sarum, contains an entirely different office for the feast. It is placed in the proper of saints at November 9th, though not included in the kalendar. Second, the corresponding mass appears in the Arbuthnott missal for November 9th, under the rubric 'In festo Sancti Salvatoris'.[1] The collect is identical with that of the Aberdeen office. The epistle and gospel are taken from those of the Ember seasons. The mass is

Dedication of the Basilica of the Saviour on November 9th. But there is no office for either. The 1534 Roman breviary specifies the common office of the dedication of a church for November 9th. Ebner, 231, notes a MS. Roman missal, probably for Italian Augustinian use, of 1506 which has a supplement in the original hand including masses for the Presentation, Holy Name, Five Wounds, and 'Iconia'.

[1] On p. lxix of the preface of the *Arbuthnott Missal*, the editor, A. P. Forbes, gives what is probably the fullest treatment this feast has had in English: 'There is on the 9th of November a feast of S. Salvator, commemorating the miraculous bleeding of a crucifix pierced by the Jews. This occurs neither in the Sarum nor in the York nor in the Hereford. It has a fine sequence, beginning "Christo vero salvatori". On this subject the Very Rev. Dr. Rock writes "The mass 'in festo S. Salvatoris' is a great liturgical curiosity . . .".' I have not been able to find this state-

not constructed on such obviously derivative lines as the Roman one. There are no verbal connections whatever between the two masses, as there are none between the Sarum and Aberdeen offices.

The hymns of the Aberdeen office[1] seem unique to it, and of not much literary merit. Those in the Sarum office are of somewhat greater interest. The vespers and matins hymns, 'Nos imago Trinitatis' and 'Pange lingua gloriosi proelium certaminis / Innovatum' have been discovered only in one other place, a printed breviary of 1543 from Calahorra,[2] in the same part of Spain from which we noted a number of earlier observances of the feast. The hymn for lauds, 'In passione Domini', is taken from the office of the Passion composed by Bonaventure, perhaps at the request of Louis IX.[3] It is interesting that this hymn was in some places used, at compline and at matins, for the feast of the Crown of Thorns:[4] a further connection with the cult of the instruments of the Passion.

Another such connection is the introduction into the Aberdeen lessons of a crown of thorns as one of the indignities inflicted on the image. This is virtually the only new touch in either of the versions; and the compilers of both offices have clearly had a text of the pseudo-Athanasian sermon in front of them in composing the lessons.[5] The Sarum lessons follow the story more closely, and are better told: the story moves at a more or less even pace throughout the nine lessons, whereas the Aberdeen version is badly timed, and there is almost no room left to recount the healing miracles or the conversion of the Jews. Both versions omit a long rhetorical exhortation before the piercing of the image. In neither is there any mention of Athanasius, or of the Council.

ment of Rock's. The Arbuthnott sequence is proper to its mass, and unique for this missal.

1 'Tunc caelum horruit', 'Jesu, solamen miseris', and 'Imago lucis'.

2 *AHMA* xvi. 37–8.

3 *AHMA* l. 568–70; Bonaventure, *Omnia Opera* viii (Quaracchi, 1898), 152. This, as we have seen, is the office on which the votive office of the Compassion was modelled.

4 F. J. Mone, *Lateinische Hymnen des Mittelalters* i (Freiburg, 1853), 112; H. A. Daniel, *Thesaurus Hymnologicus* iv (Halle, 1855), 219.

5 Like, for instance, BM MS. Add. 16415, a tenth-century collection of saints' lives which begins with the story of the Beirut image. It contains neither the tradition about Nicodemus nor the establishment of the feast, and the lessons in our office could have been taken, in condensed form, out of it; but Mr. Derek Turner of the British Museum informs me that the hand is German.

Since neither of these offices has been much known, it may be instructive to look at them somewhat more closely as examples, albeit perhaps not typical ones, of later medieval liturgical composition. Both offices tell a not very sublime story at great length and with maximum elaboration; but the total effect of each, far from being boring or ridiculous, is moving and highly dramatic. The first antiphon of the Sarum office recalls again the confusion of the miracle with the dedication: 'Dedicationem Salvatoris hodie celebramus: cuncta qui gubernat protegit et refovet.' The same theme is picked up in the antiphon to the Magnificat: 'Salvatoris majestas mundum omnem sanctificat.' The story itself is first mentioned in the vespers collect ('sicut passionem ymaginis Domini salvatoris'), and in the 'Pange, lingua' hymn at matins, a rather feeble echo of its great predecessors.

The third antiphon of the first nocturn anticipates the story of the lessons in a kind of quick preview; but the first lesson begins very much as does the pseudo-Athanasian sermon, with an exhortation to consider the wonderful works of God 'in diebus nostris et circa nos'. The story proper begins with the second lesson and moves swiftly until, at the end of the third, the Jews have decided that whatever their fathers did to the Lord, they will do to the image. The responds to the lessons act as a kind of chorus (this effect would of course be enhanced when the office was said in choir), repeating or commenting on the principal features of the preceding lesson. This chorus effect is seen very clearly in the antiphons to the second nocturn, where the psalms are woven in alternately with the iterated facts of the story. The same effect is repeated throughout this nocturn, as though the chorus is not quite able to keep up with the meaning of the lessons. Indeed, by the third nocturn, the antiphons are lagging almost halfway behind, so that when the respond to the eighth lesson arrives, the chorus is at the exclamations of the confounded Jews in lesson vi: Glory to God, Father, Son and Holy Ghost. This provides a most effective setting for the exordium of lesson ix, which is of course not followed by a respond.

The impact of the Aberdeen office is similar. There is somewhat less of the deliberate rhetorical building towards a unified effect, and at times a slightly headlong quality is noticeable. The responds tend to continue the story of the lessons rather than comment on it, and sometimes they get ahead of the lessons. But there are moving passages, such as the juxtaposition of the reading of the mass gospel at matins—the story of the fig-tree which bears no fruit—with the seventh lesson, which begins 'Didicimus quam nostri maiores coronam de spinis in capite illius nazareni imposuerunt': the underlining of the faithlessness of the Jews, as the barren fig-tree which is to be judged, could hardly be more striking.

But no matter how dramatically and devotionally satisfying this office was, it did not spread. Of all the printed Sarum breviaries, only four, as we have seen, contain the office. In addition to the 'totum' editions of 1496, 1516, and 1531, 'Pars Hiemalis' of the 1497 edition, printed at Rouen by M. Morin, contains the full office, but not for November 9th. At May 24th in the kalendar, printed over in the right half of the page, we read 'Festum salvatoris'; then, at the end of the table of psalms, there is a list of feasts (which we noted in discussing the Presentation): Presentation, St. Mary of the Snows, St. Osmund, 'Festum Salvatoris', the Name of Jesus, and St. Chad. The office is given at the end of the winter sanctorale, rather than in its proper (i.e. for May 24th) place between St. Dunstan and St. Aldhelm. We might guess that the process of fitting the feast into the breviary was well under way, and we might expect to find the fully integrated office in subsequent editions. But such is not the case: the office reappears in the 1516 and 1531 books, and nowhere else.

The date given for the feast in the 1497 breviary calls attention to the peculiarity that virtually every printed Sarum missal includes the 'Festum Salvatoris' in the kalendar for May 24th, without any further notice being taken. Very little light can be shed on this mystery of the regular appearance of 'Festum Salvatoris' in the kalendars of the printed Sarum missals, and of books of hours, on May 24th. The 1474 Roman missal has 'S. Salvatoris M.' in its kalendar at May 23rd, while including 'Dedicatio basilicae salvatoris' for November 9th. Among the Sarum missals 'Festum Salvatoris' is missing only from the very earliest editions; that is, it first appears in red like the three principal 'nova festa', in the 1494 Venice edition.[1] Thereafter

[1] Influence from the early editions of the Roman missal is certainly possible; no manuscript precedent has been found in any English book. (One possible exception is Brasenose Oxf. MS. 16, a fifteenth-century Bridgettine psalter with a kalendar

it changes only in colour, black in the three editions of 1512, 1520, and 1521 (where the three other feasts are in black as well), and again in the editions from 1531 on, where the others are in red.[1] But there are only two Sarum breviaries in the kalendars of which 'Festum Salvatoris' appears. The first is the 1494 Paris totum edition, where it is set over to the right of the kalendar page for May: that is, not aligned with the other feasts. The same arrangement, as we have just seen, exists in the 1497 Rouen edition, of which only the winter part survives and which includes under the heading 'In festo Salvatoris' the office for the 'Iconia'; the subsequent pages are headed 'In festo yconie Salvatoris'. This seems to be the only case in English service books of an explicit identification between the two. At no time does the November feast of the 'Iconia' appear in a Sarum breviary kalendar, though it has been added by hand to the 1496 Rouen edition: 'Festum iconye Jhesu.'[2] Only one other kind of printed Sarum book includes the 'Festum Salvatoris' on May 24th of the kalendar: the graduals of 1527 and 1532.[3] But as in the case of the missals, there are no mass forms corresponding to the kalendar mention. Nearly all the printed books of hours and the three editions of the Sarum psalter from 1506 have only the Translation of Francis at May 24th. Neither 'Salvatoris' nor 'Iconia' appears in any York or Hereford book. Only in the Sarum and Aberdeen breviaries (and in the Arbuthnott missal) was the feast ever noticed; and there is no external evidence that it was ever observed.[4] The mystery of how it got into the English books is unsolved. One can hardly imagine what the Reformers would have made of it if it had gained any real currency in the printed service books.

from another manuscript, English and perhaps Franciscan. The kalendar, which is very late, contains one or more saints for each day, and for May 24th 'Festum Salvatoris' is given in red, after the Translation of Francis in black. The Bridgettine order, founded in 1346, is entitled 'Ordo Sanctissimi Salvatoris'.) The kalendars of the successive early editions of the Roman missal have not been collated in *Missale Romanum 1474* ii as have the other parts of the missal.

[1] In the 1557 London edition, the last to be printed, the Transfiguration is also in black as not being a greater double.

[2] I am indebted to Dr. A. T. Luttrell for inspecting the unique surviving copy of this book for me at the Edinburgh University Library.

[3] May is lacking from the kalendar of the 1507 edition, and only fragments of the 1528 edition survive.

[4] There appears to be no connection between the story and the founding of St. Salvator's College at St. Andrews by Bishop James Kennedy in 1450–8.

VII

CONCLUSION

IT seems abundantly clear that there was a liturgical phenomenon in later medieval England which can be summed up under the heading of 'nova festa'. The number of new feasts which could come under this designation is variable—we have discussed several which were in the process of becoming accepted by the time the old liturgy was suppressed—but there is a sense in which the three feasts of the Transfiguration, Visitation, and Holy Name form a recognizable (and recognized) group, which it is useful to consider as such.

We may estimate that by roughly the year 1500 in the average parish church and certainly in the great collegiate and monastic churches, three important feasts would be celebrated which had not been generally observed in, say, 1450.[1] Or, if they were not celebrated, there was probably an awareness that they ought to be (as we have seen in the case of the Eton visitation; this would be less likely to be true in the more remote districts). Examples are plentiful. In the elaborate epistle and gospel books written for the London church of St. Mary Aldermanbury in 1508 these 'nova festa' are included (curiously, the gospel for the Visitation is missing, but almost certainly by oversight since the epistle is present).[2] All Saints, Wycombe, possessed in the early sixteenth century 'iiii Queyres noted of the visitacōn of our lady iiii Queyres of the t(r)ansfiguracōn of Jhu & the mass also. Item ii Queyres de nomine Jhu'.[3] The sense of

[1] None of these feasts was included in the complaint of the Treasurer of Salisbury Cathedral in 1452 concerning the extra expenses involved by the introduction of new feasts: *Ceremonies . . . of Salisbury*, 261.

[2] BM MS. Roy. 2. B. xii (epistles), xiii (gospels). A similarly curious inconsistency occurs between Trin. Oxf. MS. 76, a (late?) fifteenth-century Sarum gospel book, which contains the gospels of the three feasts, and 77, the matching epistle book, which includes none of them. Even odder is a Florentine epistolary dated 1477 which contains the epistle for the Visitation, while the gospel is not in the matching evangeliary dated 1478. (Bodl. MS. Canon. bibl. lat. 27–8.)

[3] *The Edwardian inventories for Buckinghamshire* (Alc. ix, 1908), 138.

these three feasts as a unit existed at Ripon as late as 1540–1 (or perhaps the feasts were only introduced then, though this is somewhat difficult to believe): 'Et sol. iii thuribulariis ministrantibus in festo Nominis Jesu (et) Transfigurat. eiusdem, et Visitacione Beatae Mariae h(oc) a(nno), 9d.'[1]

It is also true, however, that each of these three feasts was in some way unique. The Visitation, as a feast of the Virgin, fell as much into that class as into the class of 'nova festa'. It is, for example, to be found more often in the kalendars of books of hours than the other two. The Transfiguration was the oldest feast; its recognition and acceptance were probably more gradual than in the other two cases, and its popular appeal would have been the smallest. The Holy Name had the greatest popular appeal—as its origin as a generously indulgenced votive mass would indicate, not to mention the numerous private devotions to the Name—but was apparently the latest to be liturgically celebrated, and the only one unbuttressed by papal promulgation.

Again, each two of these feasts stand in some way against the third. The Visitation and Holy Name, being 'major' doubles (the Transfiguration was only a 'minor' double), had octaves, and consequently made a much larger impact on the liturgical year. They would also sometimes be treated in a specially elaborate way in liturgical manuscripts, or be included in a book of select feasts; for example, they appear in the sumptuous gospel book made for Wolsey,[2] which contains only the greatest feasts (and also feasts connected with Wolsey's richly pluralistic career: SS. William for York, Cuthbert for Durham, Hugh for Lincoln, Andrew for Bath and Wells, and Frideswide for, presumably, the new foundation of Cardinal College). The Transfiguration and Holy Name, being on successive days, made a natural pair, and we have seen them frequently added to kalendars in the same hand.[3] But the Transfiguration and

[1] *Memorials of the Church of SS. Peter and Wilfrid, Ripon* iii (SS lxxxi, 1888), 287. Cf. the Yorkshire labourer's will (discussed on p. 81), which groups all three feasts under the heading 'Festa dulcissimi nominis Jesu'.

[2] Magd. Oxf. MS. 223.

[3] A further connection between the Transfiguration and the Holy Name can be seen in the woodcut initials to these feasts in the 1528 Antwerp Sarum missal and the 1531 Paris Sarum breviary. In both books the initial 'I' of 'In nomine meo', the introit to the mass of the Holy Name, is illustrated by a woodcut of the Transfiguration. (This does not appear in Procter and Wordsworth's edition of the

Visitation, being older as liturgical feasts, often appear where the Name of Jesus is absent, particularly in additions to pre-fifteenth-century books.

We see, then, that these three feasts can be regarded as 'established' by the turn of the sixteenth century. 'Establishment' in this sense is a complex and variable process, of which official promulgation is only a part. The incipient feasts which we have also considered lacked any specifically English sanction, whether because there was never enough pressure of popularity to warrant it or because in the increasingly troubled years after about 1520 the impetus, and opportunity, for promulgating new liturgical observances was lacking. It appears that the promulgation by the Northern Convocation of the Visitation in 1513 was the last such piece of liturgical legislation until the imposition of the Sarum use on the entire province of Canterbury thirty years later.

Although we have seen that the Transfiguration and, to a lesser extent, the Presentation were liturgically celebrated much earlier than the fifteenth century, for the rest there is little or no evidence of liturgical observance in England before roughly 1400, and the final extirpation of the old services at the death of Queen Mary provides a conveniently sharp terminus. In this span of a little over a century and a half liturgical development (as opposed, once again, to extra-liturgical devotion) consisted almost entirely in the enrichment of the sanctorale with new feasts[1]—though some began as votive masses only and some never developed beyond that stage. It is easy—too easy—to assume that the new feasts are simply further evidence of an over-complicated and decadent system which was shortly to collapse through its own burdensomeness. But such a view is patently unjust to evidence of liturgical vitality during the period.

Things we do not know, or know enough about, prevent us from making any final assessment of the liturgical picture of later medieval England. We do not know how much the

breviary.) In the breviary, the office of the Transfiguration is headed by a different woodcut of that event. The most usual figure for the Holy Name is of the infant Jesus seated, holding an orb in his left hand and blessing a bird (a dove?) with his right.

[1] Including new feasts of saints, which have been mentioned on p. 3 but not considered in detail.

corruption or lassitude of monastic houses prevented them from playing their basic roles as liturgical centres; nor how much, if at all, this decline was also evident in secular cathedrals. We do not for the most part know how vigorous or full was the liturgical life of the many new collegiate foundations. We know only slightly more about parochial church life—for instance, that attendance at matins and vespers as well as mass was increasingly popular, or that the more literate laity were growing accustomed to following at least the scripture readings from their own books. And, to repeat what has been said before, we cannot possibly assess what the effect of printing was, not only on the standardization of liturgical texts, but also on a fundamental aspect of the whole psychology of liturgy: the ancient balance between variable and fixed elements or, for the laity, between the parts of the service they were 'supposed' to understand and the parts which it was presumably unnecessary for them to comprehend.

The matters with which we have been dealing are rather specialized, and it may be thought that these wider questions are not much illuminated by them. But surely knowing more about the way in which liturgical observances change and develop helps us to understand better the whole of later medieval spirituality. 'Spirituality' is too often considered to be virtually synonymous with private devotion, and to be divorced from what goes on in church. If in the case of the Holy Name popular devotion (especially the devotion of that admittedly rather unrepresentative figure, the Lady Margaret) helped to bring about liturgical celebration, it is equally true that the various considerations of ecclesiastical politics which were primarily responsible for observance of the Visitation led to a genuine enrichment of what may be regarded as the soundest type of Marian devotion; and that the self-aggrandizing of Callistus III (if that was his principal motive in promoting the Transfiguration from its state of sporadic observance) made universal in the Western church a devotion of great potential value and appeal, as it had long been in the East. Of the incipient observances connected with the cult of the Passion (Five Wounds, Crown of Thorns, Virgin's Compassion) it is somewhat more difficult to speak confidently; it may be that there is some limit to the number of observances connected with the

Passion which a healthy corporate spirituality—which is one of the things liturgy is about—can tolerate. Of the Presentation and the 'Iconia Domini' it is possible to say flatly that they were somewhat precious: self-conscious and artificial observances based on legends of no very great importance (but not the less interesting to us for that).

The preceding statements reflect value judgements which can be rejected without altering the importance of inquiring as closely as possible into the liturgical life of past ages. Indeed, the study of liturgical history has so often been undertaken in the course of editing a text, or compiling the customs of a particular church or order, or writing what is essentially the history of liturgical legislation, that it is not always sufficiently clear that the history of worship offers an important key to the history of spirituality and also to the history of ideas. Analysis of the content of the variable forms at each service can be as revealing as the study of the outlines of the rites themselves. Much of the groundwork for a more thorough study of medieval liturgy has been completed, though much more remains to be done, particularly in the classification and description of manuscripts on a wider scale than the cataloguing of individual collections will allow. When more has been done, it will be seen that the complexities of liturgical development provide valuable illumination for the 'spiritual history' of a period.

INDEX OF MANUSCRIPTS CITED

(All page references are to the notes.)

INDEX

(Authors and works included in the table of abbreviations have, with few exceptions, not been indexed.)

PRINTED IN GREAT BRITAIN
AT THE UNIVERSITY PRESS, OXFORD
BY VIVIAN RIDLER
PRINTER TO THE UNIVERSITY